Networks of Power:

Organizational Actors at the National, Corporate, and Community Levels

SOCIAL INSTITUTIONS AND SOCIAL CHANGE

An Aldine de Gruyter Series of Texts and Monographs

EDITED BY

Peter H. Rossi
Michael Useem
James D. Wright

Networks of Power:

Organizational Actors at the
National, Corporate, and
Community Levels

Robert Perrucci and Harry R. Potter, Editors

49-1190

Aldine de Gruyter
New York

About the Editors

Robert Perrucci is Professor of Sociology, Department of Sociology and Anthropology, Purdue University. He has published numerous articles and ten books on topics related to the interplay of technology and society, work and occupations, and complex organizations. He is co-author of *Plant Closings: International Context and Social Costs* (Aldine de Gruyter, 1988).

Harry R. Potter is Associate Professor of Sociology, Purdue University. He has published numerous articles for professional journals, and is presently investigating social change and social structure, and the role of law, citizen participation, and environmental policy in these areas. Dr. Potter's research also includes the decision-making process in the determination of sites for such controversial facilities as toxic waste dumps.

ALDINE DE GRUYTER
A Division of Walter de Gruyter, Inc.
200 Saw Mill River Road
Hawthorne, New York 10532

Library of Congress Cataloging-in-Publication Data
Networks of power : organizational actors at the national, corporate, and community levels / [edited by] Robert Perrucci and Harry R. Potter.
  p. cm. — (Social institutions and social change)
  Proceedings of a conference held Oct. 10–11, 1986 at Purdue University, sponsored by the Dept. of Sociology and Anthropology.
  Bibliography: p.
  Includes index.
  ISBN 0-202-30342-X. — ISBN 0-202-30343-8 (pbk.)
  1. Interorganizational behavior—United States—Congresses.
2. Power (Social sciences)—Congresses. 3. Decision-making, Group-
-United States—Congresses. 4. Corporate culture—United States-
-Congresses. 5. Associations, institutions, etc.—United States-
-Sociological aspects—Congresses. I. Perrucci, Robert.
II. Potter, Harry R. III. Purdue University. Dept. of Sociology
and Anthropology. IV. Series.
HM131.N455 1989
303.3—dc 19   89-1211
                                                                        CIP

Printed in the United States of America
10 9 8 7 6 5 4 3 2 1

Contents

5 Organizational Ties and Urban Growth   97
J. Allen Whitt

6 Network Perspectives and Policy Analysis: A Skeptical View   111
David A. Caputo

7 An Outsider's View of Network Analyses of Power   119
Arthur L. Stinchcombe

Preface

The importance of organizations as key actors has been receiving increasing attention in an effort to understand the structure of influence at the community, national, and global levels. Large organizations, particularly corporations and some government agencies, possess considerable resources and thus have considerable power, which may extend beyond any single community or nation-state. Linkages or networks among large organizations enhance that power to the point that they may have considerable impact on national and multinational economies and policies as they make decisions, and as they try to influence others' decisions, to achieve their goals. Those corporate decisions may not be compatible with the goals of single communities or nation-states, thus creating conflicts to which communities and nation-states may respond with new policy initiatives.

The past 15 years have seen considerable growth of scholarly work on interorganizational relations. Theory and research in the area have focused primarily on how interorganizational relations (1) facilitate resource acquisition and (2) are the basis for coalitions and collective action. With this work as background, we decided to bring together leading scholars to examine the contribution of interorganizational analysis to the study of power in three areas: national policy domains, community influence structures, and national corporate structure. The result was a conference at Purdue University on October 10–11, 1986 that was titled "Interorganizational Relations and the Study of Power." This conference was the first in a continuing series, sponsored by the Department of Sociology and Anthropology, that would focus on a variety of scholarly topics.

The conference was structured around four key papers by Edward Laumann and David Knoke, Eugene Johnsen and Beth Mintz, Joseph Galaskiewicz, and J. Allen Whitt. Reactions to the papers were presented by David Caputo and Arthur Stinchcombe.

As co-organizers of the conference and co-editors of this volume, we would like to thank the Department of Sociology and Anthropology at Purdue University for providing funding. The University Editor's office developed a conference brochure and the Social Research Institute distributed it to schools in our region and scholars across the country who are interested in the topic. We extend our appreciation to Denise Howard and Kay Solomon for preparation of the final manuscript and to Mary Perigo for coordinating arrangements for conference participants and visiting scholars.

Robert Perrucci and *Harry R. Potter*

List of Contributors

David A. Caputo
Professor of Political Science
Dean of Humanities, Social Sciences, and Education
Purdue University
West Lafayette, IN

Joseph Galaskiewicz
Professor of Sociology
University of Minnesota-Twin Cities
Minneapolis, MN

Eugene Johnsen
Professor of Mathematics
University of California
Santa Barbara, CA

David Knoke
Professor of Sociology and Department Chairman
University of Minnesota
Minneapolis, MN

Edward O. Laumann
George Herbert Mead Distinguished Service Professor in Sociology
University of Chicago
Chicago, IL

Beth Mintz
Associate Professor of Sociology
University of Vermont
Burlington, VT

Arthur L. Stinchcombe
Professor of Sociology, Political Science, and Organizational Behavior
Northwestern University
Evanston, IL

J. Allen Whitt
Professor of Sociology
University of Louisville
Louisville, KY

1 The Collective Actor in Organizational Analysis

Robert Perrucci
Harry R. Potter

Interest in the sociological study of organizations in the 1940s and 1950s reflected an awareness of the significance of these social units for understanding modern society. The important case studies by Blau (1955), Gouldner (1954), and Selznick (1949) did much to stimulate research in this area. The theoretical and methodological concerns of this early work set a research agenda that emphasized the internal social structures of organizations. Anthologies edited by Merton, Gray, Hockey, and Selvin (1952) and Etzioni (1961), presenting the "state of the art" in organizational analysis, contain a heavy emphasis on such topics as goals, authority relations, decision making, and organizational change. Interestingly, when there is recognition of forces external to the organization, it is usually in connection with the "power environment of bureaucracy."

In the early 1960s, there were several efforts to conceptualize *interorganizational relations* as a subtopic within organizational analysis. Levine and White (1961) and Litwak and Hylton (1962) call attention to the importance of relationships *between* organizations for understanding the role of competition and conflict in obtaining scarce resources. The substantive matters discussed in these papers draw heavily on community settings and on the activities of health, welfare, and social service agencies. The large corporations, with their vast economic and political power, were still studied primarily within the province of the field of economics.

In the mid-1960s, the *Handbook on Organizations,* edited by James March, was published. This 28-chapter, 1247-page volume covered an extraordinary range of topics involving organizational analysis. It covered foundations and methods, a wide range of theoretical–substantive areas, specific institutions, and applications. A curious paradox in this volume is that while its index contained no mention of interorganizational phenomena, the volume contained a chapter by Arthur Stinchcombe (1965) entitled "Social Structure and Organizations." It began with the following line: "The general topic of this chapter is the relation of the society outside organization to the internal life of organizations." It was to become extremely influential in shaping sociologists' thinking on organization–environment relations.

The last 20 years has seen the establishment of interorganizational analysis as an important subdiscipline in sociology. [See Galaskiewicz (1985) and Turk

(1985) for excellent discussions of work in this area.] The perspective has been applied to a variety of topics. At the risk of filtering everything through an interorganizational lens, we would like to illustrate this way of thinking with reference to several important events in U.S. foreign policy.

In 1954, Jacobo Arbenz, president of Guatemala, was overthrown by an invading force of 200 exiles who were armed and trained by the Central Intelligence Agency (Immerman, 1982; Kinzer and Schlesinger, 1981). Arbenz, an ardent nationalist, had displeased the United States with many of his land reforms and social welfare programs, which were believed to be communist inspired. In addition, Arbenz had ordered the confiscation of unused agricultural land of the United Fruit Company, the country's largest landowner (Landes and Flynn, 1984). The concerns of the United Fruit Company about Arbenz's reforms received a sympathetic hearing from the Truman and Eisenhower administrations, due undoubtedly to the existence of extensive ties between United Fruit and government officials.

The Secretary of State, John Foster Dulles, was a former member of the Wall Street firm of Sullivan and Cromwell, not only long known for representing U.S. corporations in Latin America but also United Fruit's legal representative in Guatemala. His brother, Allen Dulles, who was director of the CIA during the overthrow of Arbenz in Guatemala, had also been a partner with the same firm.

The Assistant Secretary of State for Inter-American affairs, John Cabot, had previously been ambassador to Guatemala and was a large stockholder in United Fruit. John's brother, Thomas Dudley Cabot, was the director of the State Department's Office of International Security Affairs and had been a director and president of United Fruit (Immerman, 1982). He had also been a director of The First National Bank of Boston, which was the registrar bank for United Fruit. Another of the bank's directors was the Secretary of Commerce, Sinclair Weeks (Immerman, 1982:124).

The list of United Fruit–U.S. government ties continues, but the point has probably been made. The extensive ties among agencies of government, United Fruit, and the banking community provided ample opportunity for the flow of information and the exercise of influence over the course of U.S. policy toward Guatemala. It should also be noted that United Fruit and the U.S. State Department made sure that the American public was made sufficiently aware of the unfair treatment of United Fruit by the Arbenz government and of the dangers of communism in that country. Edward L. Bernays, United Fruit's public relations counsel, was responsible for a major campaign to publicize the communist threat in Guatemala. Bernays was successful in getting the *New York Herald Tribune* to publish a five-part series on Guatemala. After Arbenz's election, Bernays organized a fact-finding trip to Guatemala for editors and publishers. Among the publications involved were *Time, Newsweek,* the foreign editor for Scripps-Howard papers, *Nashville Banner, Cincinnati Enquirer, San Francisco Chronicle, Miami Herald,* and the *Christian Science Monitor* (Immerman, 1982:112). *The New York Times,* apparently independently of Bernays' efforts, provided their own coverage of Guatemala which portrayed the "Arbenz government as being in full partnership with the Communists" (Immerman, 1982:125).

Some 30 years later, in the 1980s, the President of the United States along with a number of agencies of government are involved in a massive effort to shape public opinion and political discourse about the U.S. policy of creating and supporting a counterrevolutionary army (the "contras") and trying to overthrow the government of Nicaragua. This anti-Sandinista campaign has apparently been effective with the World Bank and the Inter-American Development Bank, which suspended or rejected economic development programs to Nicaragua (Vilas, 1986:261). The Campaign was also effective with the U.S. Congress which generally voted funds to support the contras and constantly criticized the Sandinista government even when they opposed aid to the contras. Moreover, there are reports that during the period that Congress was considering aid to the contras, major national newspapers like *The New York Times* and *Washington Post* published numerous opinion pieces critical of the Sandinista government of Nicaragua (Chomsky, 1988).

The campaign directed against Nicaragua is more elaborate and sophisticated than that of Guatemala 30 years earlier, but the existence of a network of government agencies and private sector organizations is unmistakably the same. Mathews (1986) provides a mapping of the links and lines of coordination among a large number of organizations concerned with providing aid to the contras and with shaping public opinion on the issue (see Fig. 1.1).

Despite efforts by the government to mobilize institutional and organizational support for the contras and against the Sandinistas, public opinion polls indicated that a fairly consistent two-thirds of the American public opposed aid to the contras. The only reversal to this pattern was after Lt. Colonel Oliver North's televised personal appeal for contra aid, made during the Iran–Contra congressional hearings. There were also organized pockets of resistance to the administration's Central American policies found in a loosely connected network of grassroots political and religious groups scattered across the country.

In addition to these international cases, there are other examples of significant action being taken by such networks of organizations. One is the case of Leasco, described by Mintz and Schwartz (1985). Leasco attempted a "take over" of Chemical Bank of New York. It was rebuffed through concerted efforts by economic (banks and institutional investors) and political (state and national) actors. Another example is the network of regulatory and law enforcement agencies that worked together in the Revco drug store medicaid case. This

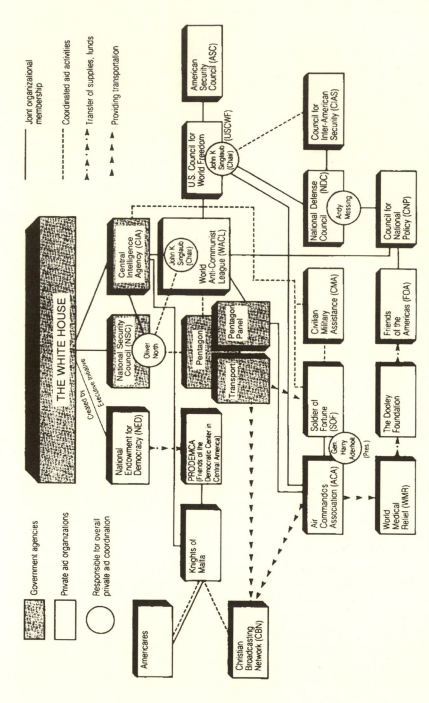

Figure 1.1. The domestic contra aid network: a pictorial view (Mathews 1986:31).

involved the Ohio State Pharmacy Board, Department of Public Welfare, Highway Patrol, and Franklin County Prosecutor's Office, each bringing their specialized but limited resources to bear on the case (Vaughan, 1983).

There are several questions that arise from these cases. The apparent inability of an elaborate network of governmental and public organizations to "penetrate" communities and primary groups and shape public opinion on the contras raises important questions about the relationship between organizations and the natural persons who are its members or citizens. Has the public become so cynical, sophisticated, or satiated with media messages that any effort by government or corporations to shape specific opinions is bound to fail? In contrast, are large organizations more effective in agenda control and influencing how issues are framed over a long period of time? Or are large organizations effective in shaping public opinion only when there are few natural persons and community-level groups with contrary messages?

This brief look at U.S. foreign policy initiatives in Central America and other cases can be used to identify a number of important themes in interorganizational analysis that underlie many of the chapters in this book. These themes reflect not only the changing structure of modern industrial societies but also the need for a new set of theoretical and methodological frameworks for understanding the emerging structures.

The first theme is a recognition of the growing scope and centrality of organizations in the life of contemporary society. The realms of private, communal, and informally arranged activities have given way to formally coordinated, national organizations. A defining feature of traditional–communal society is that important social activities often cannot be distinguished from the persons carrying out those activities. Examples include mom and pop businesses, solo private practice physicians, local newspapers, and neighborhood associations. The identities of the natural person, the organization, and the activity are often fused and are an integral part of community life. In contemporary society, there are a growing number of organizations that compete for our attention in everyday life. This is revealed in data reported by Ronald Burt (and cited in Coleman, 1982:12) on the front page attention given to organizations and to natural persons in *The New York Times*. Between 1876 and 1972, the proportion of attention given to natural persons as the subject or object of actions declined from about 40 to 20%, while space for corporate actors (i.e., organizations) increased.

The way in which contemporary organizations carry out their activities has serious implications for the health and welfare of most Americans. Decisions made at corporate and organizational levels can affect a community's economy, health care, educational opportunities, environmental pollution, and social services to name only a few things related to life chances and quality of life.

The second theme involves the concentration of economic resources in a relatively small number of giant corporations and financial institutions. Although there are over 200,000 industrial corporations in the United States, the largest 100 corporations hold over 50% of all industrial corporate assets (Dye, 1979). The top 50 commercial banks hold about 66% of all the banking assets held by some 14,500 banks. A similar concentration of economic resources can be found in transportation, utilities, and communication corporations. Many of these giant corporate actors have extensive investments in more than one nation and are among the worlds largest multinational corporations. The foreign investments of multinationals often, as in the case of United Fruit, lead them to play a role in shaping the political and economic structures of their host countries (Petras and Morley, 1975; U.S. Senate Select Committee, 1975).

The existence of vast economic resources in corporations headed by a small elite group of decision makers raises questions about how these resources will be used and who will be involved in making such decisions. It also raises questions about the relationship between the upper executives of large corporations, who act as their agents, and the corporations themselves. There are two theoretical approaches to understanding the role of organizational leaders. In the case of resource dependence theory, organizations need to control their environment in order to obtain needed resources and advance their interests. Organization leaders are viewed as agents of organization interests (Palmer, 1983). In contrast, social class theory views organizational leaders as promoting class-wide interests through the organizations they control (Useem, 1979). Leaders are selected to high positions because of their class backgrounds and their ability to become part of a diffuse set of social relationships with other leaders, thereby advancing class-wide interests (Useem and Karabel, 1986).

These two theories have important implications for understanding the behavior of large organizations and for developing social policy to control or regulate their activities.

The third theme is concerned with the role of the state in advanced societies. The state is not simply an arena or setting where conflicting interests (e.g., corporate and working classes) are managed or mediated. In the United States, there has been a centralization of power in the state that parallels the concentration of economic power. The size and expanded role of the federal government is seen in economic, social, and military programs and spending. In 1929, total government expenditures as a percentage of national income was about 12%. In 1976, the figure was almost 42% (U.S. Department of Commerce, 1977). The fiscal and monetary policies of the government are used to provide price stability, regulate unemployment, and minimize major ups and downs in the economy. The government is also heavily involved in education, funding for research and development, farm subsidies, and health care, to name but a few. Moreover, the United States seems to be operating on a permanent wartime economy, as measured by the size of our military forces and the level of defense spending.

In short, since World War II, the state has emerged as a major actor in both domestic and national economies. And precisely because of the growing role of the state, and the resources it controls, there are increased efforts to use the state to advance private interests. The passive role of the state in the early part of the century and its growing significance in recent years parallels research evidence indicating that upper class participation in government was modest in earlier years (Baltzell, 1964), but quite extensive in recent years. Domhoff (1967) and Mintz (1975) report extensive upper class involvement in cabinet positions (e.g., secretaries of state, defense, and treasury), and the pattern is consistent over time (between 1897 and 1973) and regardless of Democratic or Republican presidents.

Upper class, corporate, or working-class efforts to influence government policy will depend upon their ability to be involved in the policy formation process. This involves: (1) the universities and foundations that carry out research on important questions; (2) the policy formation groups that use research information to make recommendations to government agencies; and (3) the opinion makers in national media and special governmental commissions who develop reports and recommendations for decision makers. Involvement in this process depends upon the ability of interest groups to use their money and their personnel to penetrate the different stages in the policy formation process (Domhoff, 1979).

The fourth theme is a recognition of the role of networks of organizations, rather than single organizations, in the exercise of power. Increasingly, large and powerful organizations act to pool their resources for the purpose of influencing the policy formation process. The existence of networks of interlocked organizations or interconnected leaders is probably related to concentration of corporate and financial resources in a relatively small number of firms. With a smaller number of large corporate actors, there is greater need to take each others activities into account, thereby leading to greater information sharing and joint actions.

Analysts have identified different aspects of these emerging networks, referring to them as "social circles" (Kadushin, 1968), "inter-organizational resource networks" (Perrucci and Pilisuk, 1970), "interlocking directorates" (Mariolis, 1975; Koenig, Gogel, and Sonquist, 1979; Mizruchi, 1982), and "collective actors" (Laumann and Marsden, 1979). Whatever the differences in how networks of persons and organizations have been approached conceptually and methodologically, these efforts reflect the search for a level of analysis that mirrors the changing nature of the subject under investigation.

Organizations are increasingly involved in efforts to adapt to and control their environment. In some cases, such efforts are task related and are concerned with obtaining needed resources. In other instances, it reflects a desire to share information resulting in the formation of diffusely structured networks that perform a "business scan" function of monitoring a wide variety of business, political, and social developments (Useem, 1982).

In the foreign policy case of Guatemala described previously, the ability of United Fruit to get its concerns on the White House or State Department agendas is a reflection not simply of its power as a corporation *qua* corporation, but rather its embeddedness in elaborate networks of persons and organizations capable of shaping the reality of events in Guatemala.

A fifth and final theme concerns the relationship between organizations and the persons who are its members, employees, or customers. This relationship, as Coleman (1982) has pointed out, is characterized by asymmetry of resources and information, leaving natural persons relatively powerless in their relationship with organizations. Customers lack information about product quality and safety, but corporations use market research to learn about customer preferences and spending patterns. Students know very little about the quality of education available at different schools to which they apply, but colleges require prospective students to provide considerable personal and academic information. Workers have few alternatives when faced with a corporation that maintains hazardous working conditions or that decides to shut down and move production to a lower wage area.

The interests of customers or workers can be represented by the intervention of countervailing organizations such as consumer action groups or labor unions, but their effectiveness is often limited. The ability of large organizations to gather and disseminate information and to influence the policy process far exceeds that of citizen groups. Even labor unions, the strongest and best organized of the countervailing organizations, have had a difficult time in the 1980s offsetting the power of employers. Many workers have had to accept renegotiated contracts calling for extensive wage and benefit concessions when faced with the threat of plant closings and capital flight to low-wage labor markets.

One of the more interesting new actions developed by countervailing actors is the formation of coalitions, or networks of organizations, to apply maximum pressure on large corporations and the networks in which they are embedded. For example, Terry (1988) reports on the long struggle of farm laborers and the Farm Labor Organizing Committee (FLOC) in the midwest states to obtain collective bargaining contracts with growers and with large food processors like Campbell Foods. After repeated failures to obtain recognition, FLOC was finally successful in getting Campbell to negotiate a contract. This was the result of FLOC's corporate campaign against Campbell that started with identifying the links between the food company and other organizations (such as banks) and large shareholders. FLOC used its own linkages with other unions, church and community groups, and politicians to mobilize and direct pressure on the vulnerable links in Campbells interlocking network. Thus, FLOC directed criticism at large financial institutions like Prudential Insurance, Equitable Life Assurance, and Philadelphia National Bank for their overlapping board members with Campbell and for implicitly condoning Campbell's treatment of farm workers.

In short, a struggle that began as a confrontation of two organizations, FLOC versus Campbell, was transformed into a struggle between two interorganizational networks. This points once again to the significance of such networks as centers of influence in the corporate world and in the world of less powerful countervailing organizations of workers, citizens, or consumers, or especially to individual persons.

Many of the themes identified above are among the central concerns of chapters in this book. Moreover, the themes are elaborated in different settings, drawing attention to interorganizational processes among national corporations, within urban social structures, and at the level of national policy formation. This suggests the generality of the themes and their applicability to a wide variety of situations in which organizations and their agents form patterned relationships.

The chapters by Galaskiewicz (Chapter 4) and Whitt (Chapter 5) focus on the urban setting and are concerned with the way in which influence on community decisions is exercised. Galaskiewicz provides an examination of reserach on how interest groups mobilize resources in order to exercise influence. The complexity of this straightforward question is revealed through an examination of the resources that may be mobilized, the "actors" with an interest in mobilizing resources, and the different means by which mobilization can occur. The structure of the chapter reflects Galaskiewicz's overriding concern with whether networks of relationships involved in exercising influence reflect the interests of organizations (i.e., managers concerns with corporate survival, growth, profitability) or the shared class-wide interests of major owners of organizations and elites with extensive organizational memberships.

The chapter by Whitt uses interorganizational analysis to explain how the interplay of local political power and elites interested in economic growth shapes the nature of contemporary cities. It is suggested that attention to the question of urban growth, as a central issue confronting cities, can help to reveal the structure of influence in a community. The chapter also examines several case studies that help to deemphasize the question of "who wins" in a political struggle, suggesting instead that the focus should be on the process by which the struggle is conducted. Whitt's conclusion is that interorganizational networks play a key role in shaping a community's agenda, and although they do not always win they are the continuing centers of influence.

Chapter 2 by Laumann and Knoke describes the social organization of U.S. national energy and health domains. They focus on the interorganizational relations among peak organizations and the national government bureaucracies with programs in these two domains. In their view, the state is a system of governmental and nongovernmental groups that compete for power and legitimacy. They find a finely interwoven pattern of relations between the public and private sectors. State bureaucracies, to be successful, need to control their organizational environment, which they attempt to do by developing stable clientele networks, funding sources, and interorganizational alliances. Competing private organizations attempt to influence policy within each domain, forming coalitions and sharing resources with other organizations that share a common preference for an event outcome. It is the dynamic interaction among these contending organizations that forms the basis of policy decision making.

In Chapter 3, Johnsen and Mintz use an interorganizational approach to examine how the modern organization with dispersed ownership fits together with the enduring capitalist class. At an abstract level, their interests are similar to Galaskiewicz's, however their approach is different. They examine corporate ties and social class separately for a national, a seminational, and seven regional networks and then compare results across these networks. They find that social class connections are generally more important and may serve as a recruiting mechanism for corporate directors. At the national level, policy planning groups were almost as important as social clubs as places for face-to-face interaction of the corporate elite, however policy planning group membership was less frequent at the other two levels and is thought to play a different but important role at the seminational and regional levels.

On the Social Control of Networks

A major emphasis in the literature on interorganizational analysis, and in the chapters of this book, is on (1) how the properties of networks influence the persons or organizations that comprise the network, and (2) how networks are able to mobilize resources to influence actors and actions that are external to the network. The purpose of this section is to examine the same questions, only in reverse.

The dominant concern is one of societal control, an examination of the means by which collectively developed standards and sanctions can be applied to collective actors. This is in contrast to the usual emphasis on networks themselves as mechanisms of control. Interorganizational relations usually examine macro structures (Turk, 1985), which attempt to exercise control, for example over resources (Galaskiewicz, 1985) or provide coordination, especially in governmental programs (Hall, 1982).

In many cases, the organizations in networks are themselves large, powerful entities acting in their own self-interest. The free market capitalism perspective sees these organizations as independent, and competition among them serves as the mechanism of control with the market determining prices and less efficient firms loosing out to more efficient firms. However, this does not take into account cartels and oligopolies, that is, networks of organizations whose interests benefit from coordinated action, even over maximizing benefits to the individual firm (Roy and Bonacich, 1988).

A network's duration, or stability over time, may be an important factor with regard to social control. Some networks may be only temporary coalitions of organizations that come together for a specific, limited purpose and disband after the event or issue is over or is no longer viable. Consent may be limited only to one or a few issues, and beyond that dissent or conflict may dominate the interorganizational relations among them (Zald and McCarthy, 1987). Such coalescing, dissolving, and realigning among organizations may constitute a pluralist situation in which no concerted power base exists over time. In this case, the routine forms of social control expressed through the various interests may operate.

However, in the case of peak organizations (acting as agents for networks of similar interest organizations), or perhaps in "the enduring interests of social class" (Johnsen and Mintz, Chapter 3, this volume) duration may be much longer and effects much greater. These are the networks that are more likely to affect major decisions and also to affect what issues get on the national agenda (Laumann and Knoke, Chapter 2, this volume). The ability to control the policy agenda is a major source of power. Most important, it determines the allocation of state resources. In addition, it is the basis for regulations that may be beneficial or harmful to interests.

By controlling the agenda, and thus preventing minor organizations from obtaining state action on issues of importance to them, the major actors exercise great power which is more subtle but nonetheless effective. These minor organizations (or individuals as well) become in essence "nonplayers" in the policy game.

While social control in the sense of illegal behavior has been addressed (see, e.g., Vaughan, 1983), the examination of social control in the policy sense is much less frequent. How long was there evidence of child abuse, homelessness, mine safety hazards, and pollution of air, land, and water before they became agenda items? How effective has that legislation been? There are publicly controversial newer issues, like the distribution of organs for transplants, surrogate parenting, or "orphan" drugs, that are receiving some attention. But what of other, less known, more localized issues? Do these issues simply get omitted from the policy agenda?

A second topic is whether it is useful to consider regulatory behavior by government agencies as a form of interorganizational relations. It clearly differs from the voluntary forms of relations, such as interlocking directors. Vaughan's (1983) study of corporate crime describes the relations among law enforcement agencies in taking action against a single firm. But we propose here a broader view of how agencies and organizations within their jurisdiction interact at both the formal and informal levels.

In this view, both agencies and organizations have goals and procedures for achieving them. Agencies and organizations within their jurisdiction are significant components of each others' environments. The regulatory process, including the agency, legislative bodies, and the courts, may play an important part in what the organization's procedures are, from production processes to accounting procedures. Similarly, organizations need to be familiar with the agencies procedures.

This broad, general description plus the mandatory nature of regulation might suggest that interorganizational relations would be similar across a broad variety of agency–organization settings. This seems unlikely. First, the regulatory part of such interactions is often more complex, involving several organizations (Vaughn, 1983). In addition, an agency may have more than one basis for interaction, involving both programs and regulation (Potter and Schweer, 1988). Second, previous research has suggested diverse concepts for understanding interactions that take place in the regulatory process. Kaufman (1960) describes the problem of the isolated, local bureaucrat/professional and his/her interaction with the local community as capture (by local interests) versus conformity (to professional standards). Handler (1986) describes the important role deception plays in agency actions at the local level.

Regulation is, of course, one form of social control. As such this is an extension of our first concern about how to control networks. However, interorganizational relations research could more specifically examine this connection. A comprehensive picture would examine the process by which regulations come into being and are carried out. Simply put, the actors include the advocates and opponents of the regulations, the legislative body that enacts it, the administrative agency that implements it, often the courts that interpret it, and those who benefit or are sanctioned by it. Most research gives a static picture of some segment of this process. Perhaps because this process is often long we have little longer term data. Comparisons of the networks of advocates and opponents of legislation with the networks of beneficiaries and those sanctioned would be very informative. This would begin to piece together larger patterns of power and interorganizational relations analytically without having to rely on the case study method.

The third concern involves the extensiveness of interorganizational power. We do not dispute that governments and large firms can exercise substantial power. It follows, then, that others have little power. But we would ask two questions about that power: What are its boundaries and how are they maintained or changed. One aspect of this is mentioned by Laumann and Knoke (this volume, Chapter 2), that is, that major organizational actors in the national policy scene keep out minor actors. We assume these minor actors want to play the game, too.

But what about those actors who do not want to play the game? We refer not to the pluralist view of actors who get involved on other issues, but to those who do not get involved at all. One popular concept that may apply here is the "underground economy." This general concern may correspond to what Gamson (1987) calls a "blind spot" in the organizational approach to social movements, that is, the cultural or "hearts and minds" basis for giving meaning to action of participants.

In these studies of powerful networks, what assumptions do we make about the actors and the consequences of their actions for nonparticipating segments of society? Are the interests of powerful actors inherently inimical to those of others? Who benefits from their accomplishments—only the organizational participants, or are there "public interest" benefits? In addition, what assumptions do we make about these nonparticipants? Do they not want to be involved? Are they satisfied with things as they are? Do they not know how to play the game? The study of interorganizational relations has added an informative perspective to sociological knowledge. However, an examination of these issues is important to understanding organizational networks' relationships to society as a whole.

If networks of organizations or collective actors are emerging centers of power and influence in society, then new forms of social control will be required to protect societal interests. Existing means of social control, by agencies of government or private associations, are usually directed toward the actions of single organizations or by setting industry-wide standards. Networks are composed of diverse organizations that may be subject to regulatory control on matters of their particular goals and functions. But the actions and interests of the collectivity are probably unidentified within existing boundaries of regulation.

References

Baltzell, E. Digby (1964). *The Protestant Establishment: Aristocracy and Caste in America*. New York: Random House.

Blau, Peter M. (1955). *Dynamics of Bureaucracy*. Chicago: University of Chicago Press.

Chomsky, Noam (1988). *The Culture of Terrorism*, Boston: South End Press.

Coleman, James (1982). *The Asymmetric Society*. Syracuse University Press.

Domhoff, G. William (1967). *Who Rules America?* Englewood Cliffs, N.J.: Prentice-Hall.

Domhoff, G. William (1979). *The Powers That Be*. New York: Vintage Press.

Dye, Thomas R. (1979). *Who's Running America?* Englewood Cliffs, N.J.: Prentice-Hall.

Etzioni, Amitai (ed.) (1961). *Complex Organizations: A Sociological Reader*. New York: Holt, Rinehart and Winston.

Galaskiewicz, Joseph (1985). "Interorganizational relations." *Annual Review of Sociology* 11:281–304.

Gamson, William A. (1987). "Introduction." In Mayer N. Zald and John D. McCarthy (eds.), *Social Movements in an Organizational Society*. New Brunswick, N.J.: Transaction Books, pp. 1–7.

Gouldner, Alvin W. (1954). *Patterns of Industrial Bureaucracy*. Glencoe, Illinois: Free Press.

Hall, Richard H. (1982). *Organizations: Structure and Process*. 3rd edition. Englewood Cliffs, N.J.: Prentice-Hall.

Handler, Joel (1986). *The Conditions of Discretion: Autonomy, Community, Bureaucracy*. New York: Russell Sage.

Immerman, Richard H. (1982). *The CIA in Guatemala: The Foreign Policy of Intervention*. Austin, Texas: University of Texas Press.

Kadushin, Charles (1968). "Power, influence and social circles: A new methodology for studying opinion makers." *American Sociological Review* 33:685–699.

Kaufman, Herbert (1960). *The Forest Ranger: A Study of Administrative Behavior*. Baltimore: Johns Hopkins Press.

Kinzer, Stephen, and Schlesinger, Stephen (1981). *Bitter Fruit: The Untold Story of the American Coup in Guatemala*. Garden City, N.Y.: Doubleday.

Koenig, Thomas, Gogel, Robert, and Sonquist, John (1979). "Models of the significance of interlocking corporate directors." *American Journal of Economics and Sociology* 38:173–186.

Landes, David, and Flynn, Patricia (1984). "Dollars for dictators: U.S. aid in Central America and the Caribbean." In R. Burbach and P. Flynn (eds.), *The Politics of Intervention: The United States in Central America*. New York: Monthly Review Press, pp. 133–161.

Laumann, Edward O., and Marsden, Peter V. (1979). "The analysis of oppositional structures in political elites: Identifying collective actors." *American Sociological Review* 44:713–732.

Levine, Sol, and White, Paul E. (1961). "Exchange as a conceptual framework for the study of interorganizational relationships." *Administrative Science Quarterly* 5:583–601.

Litwak, Eugene, and Hylton, Lydia F. (1962). "Interorganizational analyses: A hypothesis on coordinating agencies." *Administrative Science Quarterly* 6:395–420.

March, James G. (ed.) (1965). *Handbook on Organizations*. Chicago: Road McNally.

Mariolis, Peter (1975). "Interlocking directorates and control of corporations: The theory of bank control." *Social Science Quarterly* 56:425–439.

Mariolis, Peter, and Jones, Maria H. (1982). "Centrality in corporate interlock networks: Reliability and stability." *Administrative Science Quarterly* 27:571–584.

Mathews, Robert (1986). "Sowing the dragon's teeth: The U.S. war against Nicaragua." *NACLA Report* 20:13–40.

Merton, Robert K., Gray, Ailsa P., Hockey, Barbara, and Selvin, Hanan C. (eds.) (1952). *Reader in Bureaucracy*. New York: Free Press.

Mintz, Beth (1975). "The president's cabinet, 1897–1972: A contribution to the power structure debate." *Insurgent Sociologist* 5:131–148.

Mintz, Beth, and Schwartz, Michael (1985). *The Power Structure of American Business*. Chicago: University of Chicago Press.

Mizruchi, Mark S. (1982). *The American Corporate Network 1904–1974*. Beverly Hills, Calif.: Sage.

Palmer, Donald. "Broken ties: Interlocking directorates and intercorporate coordination." *Administrative Science Quarterly* 28:40–55.

Perrucci, Robert, and Pilisuk, Marc (1970). "Leaders and ruling elites: The interorganizational bases of community power." *American Sociological Review* 35:1040–1057.

Petras, James, and Morley, Morris (1975). *The United States and Chile*. New York: Monthly Review Press.

Potter, Harry R., and Schweer, Harlan M. (1988). "Organizational networks and political influence: Passage and implementation of the 'Clean Water Act.' " Paper presented at the annual meetings of the American Sociological Association, Atlanta.

Roy, William G., and Bonacich, Philip (1988). "Interlocking directorates and communities of interest." *American Sociological Review* 53:368–379.

Selznick, Philip (1949). *TVA and the Grass Roots*. Berkeley: University of California Press.

Stinchcombe, Arthur L. (1965). "Social structure and organizations." James G. March (ed.), *Handbook on Organizations*. Chicago: Rand McNally, pp. 142–193.

Terry, James L. (1988). *The Political Economy of Migrant Farm Labor and the Farmworker Movement in the Midwest*. Ph.D. dissertation, Purdue University.

Turk, Herman (1985). "Macrosociology and interorganizational relations: Theory, strategies, and bibliography." *Sociology and Social Research* 69:487–500.

U.S. Department of Commerce (1977). *The National Income and Product Accounts of the United States*. Washington, D.C.: U.S. Government Printing Office.

Useem, Michael (1979). "The social organization of the American business elite and participation of corporate directors in the governance of American institutions." *American Sociological Review* 44:553–572.

Useem, Michael (1982). "Classwide rationality in the politics of managers and directors of large corporations in the United States and Great Britain." *Administrative Science Quarterly* 27:199–226.

Useem, Michael, and Karabel, Jerome (1986). "Pathways to top corporate management." *American Sociological Review* 51:184–200.

U.S. Senate Select Committee to Study Governmental Operations with Respect to Intelligence Activities (1975). *Covert Action in Chile, 1963–1973*. Washington, D.C.: U.S. Government Printing Office.

Vaughan, Daine (1983). *Controlling Unlawful Organizational Behavior: Social Structure and Corporate Misconduct*. Chicago: University of Chicago Press.

Vilas, Carlos M. (1986). *The Sandinista Revolution: National Liberation and Social Transformation in Central America*. New York: Monthly Review Press.

Zald, Mayer N., and McCarthy, John D. (1987). *Social Movements in an Organizational Society*. New Brunswick, N.J.: Transaction Books.

2 Policy Networks of the Organizational State: Collective Action in the National Energy and Health Domains*

Edward O. Laumann
David Knoke

The executive director of a major petroleum industry trade association was leafing through the *Federal Register,* his daily ritual of scanning the Washington scene. Buried in the fine print was an apparently innocuous announcement by the Federal Aviation Administration (FAA) of its intent to promulgate new regulations that would require detailed flight plans to be filed by pilots of noncommercial aircraft. Recently, several planes had gone down, and search-and-rescue efforts had been hampered by lack of information on the pilots' intended routes. The trade association director muttered, "We've got a problem," and spent a frantic morning on the phone alerting his group's membership to apply pressure on the FAA to set aside the regulation. The executive realized that, once detailed flight plans were on record with the FAA, the open-disclosure provisions of the Freedom of Information Act would allow anyone to learn where his member companies' planes were flying on their aerial explorations for oil, gas, and minerals. The alert director's quick mobilization of collective response saved the corporations potentially millions of dollars of secret data that might have fallen into the laps of their competitors.

This incident dramatically encapsulates several important features of state policymaking: the centrality of large formal organizations; the significance of policy interests in narrowly focused events; the great value of timely and trustworthy information; the activation of policy participants through communication networks; and the mobilization of influence resources to bear upon the formal authorities. State policies are the product of complex interactions among governmental and nongovernmental organizations, each seeking to influence the collectively binding decisions that have consequences for their interests. This chapter provides an overview of a 5-year study of American energy and health policymaking, with particular emphasis on social structure, decision participation, and influence over outcomes. We have developed new analytic perspectives and

*Excerpted from Chapters 1, 12, and 14 of Edward O. Laumann and David Knoke, *The Organizational State: Social Choice in National Policy Domains.* Madison, Wisconsin: University of Wisconsin Press, 1987.

empirical measures with the view of strengthening our systematic understanding of these complex processes of national decision making.

In this chapter, we shall first characterize the variety of approaches that have been proposed to guide the study of state or elite decision making, noting where our approach departs from existing strategies of inquiry to achieve what we believe to be a more theoretically sophisticated and empirically faithful model. We are primarily concerned with problems of the levels of analysis in terms of which we must proceed and with the innovation of being systematically explicit about the joint analysis of actors and events in a system of action.

Here we lay out a theoretical framework of sufficient generality to analyze the variety of action systems. We hope to convince the reader of the model's general utility by demonstrating its efficacy in generating empirical insights in two highly distinctive and unrelated political arenas. The empirical analysis of these two policy domains, energy and health, with reference to the 1970s and to the Carter administration (1977–1980), in particular, are described in detail in Laumann and Knoke (1987).

Succinctly put, our orienting framework is *a set of consequential corporate actors,* each possessing (1) variable *interests* in a range of *issues* in a national policy domain and (2) relevant mobilizable *resources.* These actors are *embedded* within communication and resource–exchange *networks* (Marsden and Laumann, 1977; Granovetter, 1985). The flows of specialized communications and resources among the actors enable them to monitor, and to communicate their concerns and intentions, in relevant decision-making *events* that, in turn, have consequences for their interests. Features of these events, both as unique historical occurrences and in their interrelationships, have critical import for explaining the behavior of individual actors and their interaction. Figure 2.1 graphically depicts the model.

Other State Policy-Making Approaches

Our project departs in important ways from other research approaches to state and elite policymaking by political scientists and sociologists. In this section, we briefly sketch four contexts against which to view our analysis of the social organization of the state.

Recent controversies have swirled around Marxist-inspired analyses of the economic–class basis of the modern state (Miliband, 1969; Poulantzas, 1973; Gold, Lo, and Wright, 1975; Offe and Ronge, 1975; Therborn, 1976; Block, 1977; Wright, 1978; Skocpol, 1980). Instrumentalist explanations argue that state policies are determined by the class interests of capitalists and their agents. Structuralist accounts accord the state greater autonomy, depicting policy decisions as reflecting the outcome of struggles between capitalist and working

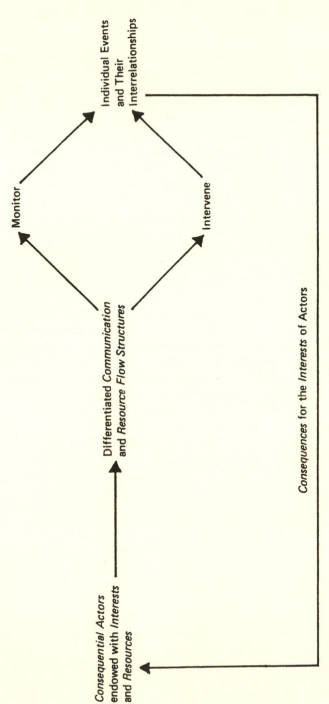

Figure 2.1. The general model.

classes or partially determined by social and political forces operating within the state structure itself. Although much of this dispute is conducted at a fairly abstract level, a few empirical efforts have examined the implications of these perspectives. Analyses have addressed the micro level of state manager–class composition (Dye, 1976) and the macro level, the latter through highly aggregated time series of policy outputs (Griffin, Devine, and Wallace, 1982; Hicks and Swank, 1984) or detailed historical case studies (Domhoff, 1978; Skocpol, 1979, 1980). None of these analyses tracks states policymaking at the level of organizational populations laying claim to governmental authority on behalf of their interests. While our project cannot elucidate the class basis of the American state, it cuts directly into that black box to reveal a complex set of interacting private and public institutions. We see policies as resulting from conflicts and contradictions among these organizational players, rather than reflecting the monolithic rationality and clarity of class interests implied by many Marxist images. By studying organizations participating in many policy events across domains, we hope to reveal the underlying social structure and dynamic of state policymaking. Perhaps these findings will add substantive fuel to Marxist theoretical debates, despite the differences in conceptual languages.

A second analytic approach conceives of the state in terms of elites whose interests are more organizationally derived than class-oriented (Field and Higley, 1980; Knoke, 1981; Heinz and Laumann, 1982; Burton and Higley, 1984). Mills' (1956) now classic image of an unaccountable business–government–military power elite dominating the state inspired empirical attempts to identify the players and map their relationships (e.g., Domhoff, 1978; Barton, 1975; Dye, 1976; Moore, 1979; Useem, 1979, 1984). Much of this research takes the individual as its unit of analysis, tracing career patterns of recruitment to top command posts or delineating discussion networks among core actors (e.g., interlocking corporate directorates). Few studies offer more than anecdotal illustrations of how elite structures affect policymaking activities (but see Laumann and Pappi, 1976; Laumann, Galaskiewicz, and Marsden, 1978; Galaskiewicz, 1979; Knoke, 1981; Perrucci and Pilisuk, 1970, for analyses involving local community elites). Although our project shares the concern of research on elite structures for mapping communication networks, we see organizations rather than natural persons as the core actors at the level of the national state. We further treat network structure as antecedent to policy–event participation and its consequences. Thus, we seek to apply principles of elite social organization in more comprehensive directions.

A third context within which to view our project is the interest group tradition of pluralist political science. Spurred by the explosion of activity in Washington since 1970, recent analyses have concentrated on the origins, prevalence, policy interests, resource endowments, and strategies of those associations and corporate actors as they seek to influence federal policy decisions (Walker, 1983;

Schlozman and Tierney, 1983; Berry, 1984). Much of this research is descriptive, and more needs to be learned about how interest groups pursue their policy objectives. Theoretical explanations of the pressure-group system too often emphasize the more formalized aspects of legislation (e.g., "cozy triangles" among executive agencies, Congressional subcommittees, and clientele; see Gais, Peterson, and Walker, 1984) to the relative neglect of less proximate causes (Ripley and Franklin, 1980:4–7; Burstein, 1981; Hayes, 1979; McFarland, 1983). Yet, as Salisbury (1984) so cogently argues, the recent dominance of such institutions as corporations and local governments over mass membership associations in Washington interest representation requires substantial revisions in both descriptive and theoretical accounts of state policymaking. Our project was designed, along with a parallel study of Washington representatives (Heinz, Laumann, Nelson, and Salisbury, 1982; Laumann and Heinz, 1985; Nelson, Heinz, Laumann, and Salisbury, 1987), to develop a more sociologically informed approach to interest group behavior. We stress the centrality of network structures among organized interest groups for the exchange of timely policy information and politically useful material resources essential to coalition formation, influence mobilization, and bargaining–negotiation processes that ultimately create state policies. In many ways, our emphasis on impacted information and the need to devise governance structures to contain opportunistic behavior runs parallel to that of Williamson's (1975; 1985) transaction cost analysis of economic institutions.

The final approach to which we contrast our project is corporatism. Like pluralism, corporatism gives special attention to organized interests and their relations to the state. Schmitter's definition stressed the "intermediation" function that groups play in a societal corporatist system in which "the constituent units are organized into a limited number of singular, compulsory, noncompetitive, hierarchically ordered and functionally differentiated categories" (Schmitter, 1979:13). Corporatism is most fully developed in European liberal democracies, where peak associations are directly incorporated into governmental deliberations, in return for controlling their fractious mass bases. Most scholars agree that the United States lacks corporatist attributes (Wilson, 1982). Still, the identification of autonomous organizations as key state actors and the insistence that state policies can be understood as a series of negotiations among interest groups are compatible with our own perspective.

From the broad sweep of political sociology and economy, our fundamental theoretical stance may best be characterized as a multiple elite (Knoke, 1981:286–288) or managerial perspective (Alford and Friedland, 1985:161–268). Eschewing both pluralistic individualism and Marxist class approaches, we conceive of the modern industrial polity as a complex of formal organizations in conflict with one another over the collective allocation of scarce societal resources. Neither aggregates of persons nor agents of class interests, the large bureaucratic state organizations are effective instruments of domination for those elites who can command their authority. Using power relations within and interorganizational networks among them, state managers and interest group leaders struggle to mobilize political resources that shape public policies beneficial to their organizations' objectives, including survival of the power structure itself (Alford and Friedland, 1985:25).

From the managerial elite perspective, the national state is neither a structure for capitalist class rule nor a neutral umpire adjudicating between competing claims of social groups. Rather, the state is an autonomous social formation whose strategies emerge from the basic organizational imperatives of coping with environmental uncertainties, resource scarcities, and sociolegal constraints (Knoke, 1981:228; see Aldrich, 1979, and Scott, 1981, for discussions of organizational autonomy and dependency in strategic choice conditions). The historical creation of the liberal democratic state—involving greater structural differentiation, increased control over societal resources, and expanded intervention into the economy and society—was accompanied by a parallel transformation of social segments into organized interest groups (e.g., Truman, 1951; Garson, 1978; Walker, 1983; Schlozman and Tierney, 1983). In attempting to maximize their legitimacy and autonomy, state bureaus created stable networks of clienteles, funding sources, and interbureau alliances. The boundaries between the public sector and private interest groups became blurred in the policymaking process (Alford and Friedland, 1985:436).

As state entities took on increasingly significant regulatory functions, dominant interests outside the state sought to secure continuous access to these new centers of power (McConnell, 1966; McNeill, 1978). Interdependent and reciprocal relations between state and private organizations jointly created the modern polity of large-scale bureaucratic hierarchies that centralized increasingly vast amounts of power. Ultimately, only efficient, resource-rich organized interests could gain access to the state managerial elites, as poor and unorganized social groups were relegated to sporadic challenges (Gamson, 1975; Tilly, 1978). Even those interest groups nominally based on mass membership and support—labor unions, political parties, trade associations, voluntary organizations—became dominated by oligarchic elites that controlled the expression of public opinion and participation in their ranks (Michels, 1962; Salisbury, 1984). Thus, the appropriate unit of analysis for studies of policy formation is not the state understood in the institutional sense, but the state as a collection of policy arenas incorporating *both* governmental and private actors (cf. Parsons, 1969).

A Model for Analysis

Two assumptions underlie the research design. First, we assume that corporate entities—such as trade associations, professional societies, labor unions, public interest groups, government bureaus, and congressional committees—are the key state policy domain actors. Natural persons are important only insofar as they act on behalf and at the behest of these collectivities [1]. Second, we adopt a social choice perspective, which assumes that supraindividual structural arrangements among these corporate entities must be taken into account in formulating an adequate explanation of policy domain event participation. These two assumptions jointly guide the following specification of our analytic model.

Policy Domains

In Parsons' (1951:19) succinct definition, a *social system* is a "plurality of actors interacting on the basis of a shared symbol system." Membership in any social system under analysis is substantively defined by a criterion of mutual relevance and common fate that stipulates the basis on which members are to take each other into account in their actions. That is, the basis of their mutual relevance to one another or their common orientations to some shared reference point (such as the production of coal for market) serves to mediate their interdependence. Simply put, a *policy domain* is the substantive focus of concern of policy initiatives and debate. More formally, a *policy domain* is a subsystem "identified by specifying a substantively defined criterion of mutual relevance or common orientation among a set of consequential actors concerned with formulating, advocating, and selecting courses of action (i.e., policy options) that are intended to resolve the delimited substantive problems in question" (Knoke and Laumann, 1982:256). A national policy domain is therefore a set of actors with major concerns about a substantive area, whose preferences and actions on policy events must be taken into account by the other domain participants. Numerous policy domains exist in the modern state. Examples include agriculture, housing, education, civil rights, health care, space exploration, law enforcement, national defense—indeed, all arenas into which governmental authority has intruded. Once a substantive criterion is specified, the researcher is in a position to define the core set of actors. Note that this criterion may change over time and even across the set of actors, transforming the definition of what is meant by a particular policy domain with consequent implications for the delimitation of its constituent membership.

To illustrate the point, today we might construe a health matter as referring to any phenomenon affecting the physiological, psychological, or health-related social well-being of an individual or group of individuals. Encompassing mental health issues, such a construction reflects a much more inclusive definition than would have been accepted by most major actors in the policy domain 30 years ago. The identification of this domain is subject to the further restriction that the relevant health policy options include only those currently considered permissible for either the federal government or private organizations with nationally oriented clienteles. Similarly, a national energy policy domain is delineated by the set of all policy options involving the production and allocation of physical power resources that are seriously considered by the federal government and the major private organizations with national markets or supporters [2].

The active participants in a policy domain include all consequential organizations that have responsibility for directing, coordinating, or otherwise controlling the creation and distribution of domain values (symbolic or material) pertaining to the subsystem's primary function or to related externalities that are thereby engendered. An organization's consequentiality in a particular domain is established by the extent to which its disclosed intentions and actions are taken into account in the actions of other domain participants. Of particular significance is the set of organizations that occupies the dominant structural positions in the subsystem from which influence over collective decision making can be exercised. This set comprises the elite or core organizations of the policy domain.

Delineating Domain Membership

For all practical purposes, the members of a national policy domain are complex formal organizations—such as corporations, confederations, commissions, and committees—rather than natural persons acting in their own right. But such corporate bodies rarely are wholly engaged in policy direction for a given subsystem. Only certain organizational components, particularly those at the executive level, participate in a domain.

We have already noted that the basic analytic criterion determining whether an organization belongs to a subsystem's policy domain is the standard of relevance or fate whereby actors take each other into account in their actions (Knoke and Laumann, 1982). This criterion of mutual relevance effectively excludes any actors whose actions or potential actions are inconsequential in shaping binding collective decisions for the subsystem. Actors with trivial capacities to affect the actions of domain policymakers thus may be safely ignored by both elite members and analysts. Mere inaction, however, is an insufficient clue to marginality, since some consequential actors, without any overt action on their part, can have their interests taken into account through the reactions of other core members who anticipate their interests in particular policies.

The boundaries between actors in the policy domain and the more peripheral members of a subsystem are never rigidly drawn. On the contrary, membership in a policy domain is a continuing collective social construction by the domain actors. Membership is the outcome of continuous negotiations between the consequential actors currently forming the elite, who seek to impose their preferred definitions and requirements for inclusion, and various excluded nonelite actors, who seek the right to participate in collective decision making for the subsystem as a whole.

The specific steps we followed to identify the core actors in the energy and health domains involve counting the frequency of occurrences in national news media, appearances at congressional hearings, and participation in lobbying and court cases, and a final scrutiny of the list by a panel of expert insiders. The result of applying these criteria for domain membership was to identify 217 energy organizations and 156 health organizations as the elite set among which informant interviews were to be conducted. (See Laumann and Knoke, 1987, Chapter 3, for complete details on the study design.)

Structural Relations

The social structure of a policy domain refers to those stable, recurrent patterns of relationships that link consequential actors to each other and to the larger social system. Research on social networks during the past decade indicates that social structure may be usefully conceptualized in terms of the multiple types of ties among system members, the patterning of which, in turn, may be used to identify a subsystem's fundamental social positions and the roles performed by particular organizations.

Contemporary treatments of social networks view the *positions* in a system of social relations as "jointly occupied" by empirical actors (White, Boorman, and Breiger, 1976; Boorman and White, 1976; Burt, 1976, 1977; Sailer, 1978). The two prevailing techniques for identifying social positions are structural equivalence and subgroup cohesion. In the approach using the criterion of structural equivalence, two or more actors jointly occupy a structurally equivalent position to the extent that they have similar patterns of ties with other system actors, regardless of their direct ties to each other. The criterion of subgroup cohesion, on the other hand, aggregates only those actors who maintain dense mutual interactions either as "cliques" (maximally connected subsets; see Laumann and Pappi, 1976) or as "social circles" (highly overlapping cliques; see Alba and Moore, 1978). Although important conceptual and methodological differences exist between the two approaches, Burt (1978) has pointed out that the clique approach is a special case of the more general approach of structural equivalence.

Research on interorganizational relations and local community political systems suggests that three generic relationships are especially significant in identifying social structure: information transmission, resource transactions, and boundary penetration.

1. *Information transmission.* Over the course of their research on local communities, Laumann and his colleagues have increasingly emphasized the flow of information about community affairs among elite actors as the primary social network for the resolution of issues (Laumann and Pappi, 1976; Laumann et al., 1978; Galaskiewicz, 1979; Laumann and Marsden, 1982). We can

extrapolate this perspective to the national level. The social structure of a national policy domain is primarily determined by the network of access to trustworthy and timely information about policy matters. The greater the variety of information and the more diverse the sources that a consequential actor can tap, the better situated the actor is to anticipate and to respond to policy events that can affect its interests.

2. *Resource transactions*. The resource dependence model of interorganizational relations (Aldrich and Pfeffer, 1976; Benson, 1975; Cook, 1977) begins with the commonplace observation that no organization is capable of generating internally all the resources necessary to sustain itself. Major sources of essential resources, especially information, money, and authority, typically are controlled by other formal organizations. In choosing exchange partners, organizational managers try to minimize the loss of autonomy, which might lead to a takeover by the dominant partner. But supply and demand conditions, resource essentiality (Jacobs, 1974), availability of alternative partners, and other factors can conspire to force some organizations into dependent positions. In this model, an organization's power and influence in a system is a function of its position or location in the overall resource exchange networks generated out of dyadic resource exchanges (see Knoke, 1983).

3. *Boundary penetration*. The third type of actor-to-actor linkage involves relationships serving both instrumental and solidarity-maintenance functions through the shared use of personnel. The more important examples of this mode of coordination include common membership in commissions or confederations of organizations (such as a peak trade association); ad hoc coalitions to pursue limited political objectives; joint operations in research, development, or production (such as a consortium to build a gas pipeline); shared board directorships; or even simple exchanges of personnel. These practices vary along dimensions of superordination–subordination, formalization, duration, and purpose (see Williamson, 1975; 1985).

The Policy Process

What does an elite subsystem oriented to a particular policy domain do when it attempts to influence national policy? Here we shall be primarily concerned with accounting for the policy development process and only secondarily with the activities of particular organizations, although the behaviors of the latter are intrinsic to the process.

Broadly following the sequence of events outlined in Smelser's (1962) model of social change, we suggest that the paradigmatic policy process begins with the perception of some disruption or malfunction in the ongoing operations of a subsystem. Actors propose alternative interpretations of the problem and the need for collective action to deal with it. In discussing the problem, policy domain actors communicate their preferred responses to one another, to nonelite audiences, and to governing actors with the authority to make binding decisions for the subsystem. Domain actors or coalitions of actors attempt to persuade the authorities to place the issue on the governmental agenda for resolution. When an issue reaches the agenda, actors mobilize in an effort to influence the outcome of a concrete issue event, which may be part of a larger event scenario. The policy cycle is closed when the authorities select one option to deal with the precipitating policy problem. If implementation of the policy option fails to alleviate the original condition or triggers additional problems, the cycle may commence again, perhaps activating other domain actors' participation (cf. Kingdon, 1984).

We should stress here that we most certainly do not conceive of this process as an approximation of the rational-actor model of decision making so beloved by organizational theorists (compare Allison, 1971). We find much more suggestive the characteristics of the organizational decision-making process proposed by March and Olsen (1976), which stresses the fundamental ambiguities of choice at every stage as actors try to decide what to do. Characteristic ambiguities are inherent in an actor's identification of the problem, definition of the objectives it wants to achieve, and determination of the procedures whereby it proposes to accomplish them. The chief feature of this perspective to which we must pay attention is the *time-dependent nature* of the actors' searches for problems and solutions. Policy processes do not occur in a vacuum, but evolve simultaneously with many others, at various stages of completion, that compete for the *scarce* attention of domain members. This multiplicity of competing activities places significant constraints on any given policy cycle and must somehow be taken into account in the empirical analysis. The following sections elaborate key features of the approach that inform our empirical analysis.

Problem Recognition

The typical policy process starts when one or more actors label some condition as a problem or issue and draw the attention of other actors to it. The organization itself may be directly experiencing strains in its operations, or it may respond to difficulties encountered by other actors (including nonelites and participants in other subsystems) that are drawn to its attention—for example, by customer complaints or criticism in the mass media. The important point is that a subsystem condition does not become a domain issue until it is recognized as a strain problem by a consequential actor in the policy domain. Nonmembers, including academic observers, cannot meaningfully assert that a subsystem's "objective" conditions are policy issues if they are ignored by such domain actors. Indeed, one criterion of membership in a domain is the willingness of other core actors to accept an organization's assertions about what constitutes an issue.

Problem recognition is clearly a subjective conceptual activity of consequential organizations or, more precisely, by their agents in policymaking roles. Just as we emphasized that membership is a collective social construction of reality, so we argue that the recognition of conditions as public problems is a continuously constructed social phenomenon, as, indeed, is the entire policy process. Subsequent conditions may stimulate participants' retrospective reinterpretations of earlier activities as having greater or lesser relevance for a problem. Problem recognition thus takes on the flavor of a constantly modified "story," one having a beginning, middle, and end, but also, like the old newspapers in Orwell's *1984,* subject to perpetual revision as actors try to make sense of their world and their actions toward it.

Whether an "objective" condition will be labeled and accepted by other domain actors as a legitimate policy issue for subsystem action depends on the result of negotiations among domain members (see Hermann, 1969; Lyles and Mitroff, 1980; Billings, Milburn, and Schaalman, 1980). Problem recognition may be highly uncertain when conditions depart markedly from past experience or have traditionally been the province of other subsystems. For example, a major problem for the energy-domain actors during the 1970s was disagreement among themselves as to the root of the "energy crisis"—a real depletion of resources or an artificial imbalance created by governmental interference in the marketplace. Differing beliefs about the nature of the problem clearly affect the types of actors who become involved and the policy alternatives that they champion.

Option Generation

Empirically, the generation of policy options or alternatives may occur simultaneously with issue recognition, but in the proposed analytic model, option generation is a subsequent step. Indeed, in some real cases we may find that the organizations first drawing attention to an issue are not the same actors who subsequently propose various policy options or solutions aimed at eliminating or reducing the strain problem and restoring the subsystem to a new equilibrium.

A *policy option* is the empirical unit act in the policy process. It consists of a statement made by a policy domain actor that advocates that a specific action be taken, either by that actor or some other authoritative actor, with regard to a socially perceived issue. Most policy options can be cast in the form: "Organization A proposes that authority B undertake action X for reason Y." For example, in 1974, the Association of American Railroads concluded that the Nuclear Regulatory Commission safety standards for casks used to ship nuclear wastes by rail were too low and, therefore, that the Interstate Commerce Commission should change the conditions under which nuclear waste shipments were made.

A domain actor communicates to other core actors, as well as to a larger nonelite "attentive public," its preferred policy option with regard to a specific subsystem problem or issue. Other actors, either differently interpreting the defining problems or perceiving that actor A's proposed alternative might be disadvantageous for themselves or others they care about, offer alternatives to cope with the problem. To illustrate: Following the 1979 accident at the Three Mile Island nuclear power plant, some actors proposed a moratorium on new plant construction, others advocated shutting down existing plants as well, and the industry actors wanted to continue operations under tighter safety procedures.

The solutions proferred by domain actors seldom are arrived at by the ideal–typical search procedures of an abstract rational actor who systematically scans all alternatives and selects one that maximizes utility. Rather, organizational option generation more often resembles solutions in search of issues. Organizational routines and standard operating procedures dispose actors toward a stock set of solutions that can be applied across a wide range of problems (see March and Olsen, 1976).

Agenda Placement

Recognition of strain problems and communications of policy options among domain members are necessary for issues to reach the "systematic agenda" (Cobb and Elder, 1972:82; Kingdon, 1984), where the subsystem elites become aware that a condition exists requiring authoritative resolution. If the problem can be dealt with only by some component of the federal government, the next step in the policy process is to place the issue on the "governmental agenda." An *agenda* is a formal calendar or docket that specifies the order and time at which matters are to be considered before a final selection is made among the available policy options. The governmental agenda is almost always smaller and more difficult for an issue to reach than is the subsystem agenda. Despite the enormous size and specialization of the federal government, there are more problems seeking the attention of executives, legislators, and regulators than can possibly be seriously entertained in a given period. Advancement onto the governmental agenda typically requires actions by proponents of an issue alternative to increase the salience and political importance of the issue to gatekeeping authorities, particularly by mobilizing politically relevant resources, including coalitions with other actors, to influence authoritative decision makers. In the process of reaching the stage of formal consideration by authorities, an issue's policy options may have undergone considerable modification and reduction as proponents and opponents negotiate over terms. This process we refer to as *winnowing* the alternatives in preparation for moving the issue onto the agenda.

Events and Scenarios

When an issue reaches a national policy domain's agenda, its subsequent progress can be analyzed in terms of discrete events. An event occurs when a concrete proposal for authoritative action is placed before a decision-making body, such as Congress or a federal regulatory agency. An event typically involves a pro-or-con decision about a single policy option as the solution to an issue. Those actors who favor and those who oppose the particular proposal may be observed marshaling their forces to try to influence the decision outcome. Such variables as the timing of activation, the influence tactics used, and cooperative and competitive interactions among mobilized actors can be investigated. Of particular interest in our research is how the domain social structure determines the time at which core actors become involved in particular types of events.

An event in the energy domain is illustrative. On February 22, 1978, the House Interior Committee reported out a bill to promote the development of coal slurry pipelines. Such pipelines would pump a mixture of crushed coal and water from mines to the users, often over hundreds of miles. The following actors were mobilized around this event: the coal industry, electric utilities, and construction trade unions, who favored the bill's passage; the railroads, who opposed development because it would cost them lucrative coal-hauling business; and environmental groups and farmers, who opposed the project on the ground that it would deplete scarce water resources. By asking spokespeople about their organizations' actions before and after the committee reported out the bill, we reconstructed the pattern of activation on this event and related it to the social organization in this sector of the national energy domain.

Discrete events can be concatenated into larger event scenarios that may span considerable time, revealing changing configurations of actors and patterns of action. Events can be chained together because they share some logical similarities, exhibit some temporal proximity and succession, or display some causal connections. To continue the illustration, coal slurry pipeline bills were brought before Congress at least three times during the Carter administration but were never passed. At a higher level of abstraction, these pipeline events can be included in a scenario called "coal industry development" that also includes events pertaining to strip mining control and reclamation, railroad deregulation, and utility air pollution standards. The ability to aggregate discrete events into more encompassing equivalence classes gives the researcher greater flexibility in trying to understand how the social organization of a policy domain affects the policymaking process.

Authoritative Decision

We will have little to say in this chapter about this final stage in the policy process. Political scientists have exhaustively studied the procedures by which laws and regulations are authorized, primarily from an institutional perspective that stresses the motives and interests of proximate decision makers (such as senators' desires for reelection). In contrast, our research brings a distinct sociological perspective to bear on the selection of outcomes, emphasizing how the social organization of timely and trustworthy information flowing from interested core actors to the proximate authorities defines the nature of the policy debate and its outcome. We do not deny the existence, and frequently substantial importance, of processes internal to the legislative and executive decision-making organizations, but our primary focus is on the contribution of social structural variation in policy domains to an understanding of ultimate policy decisions.

Empirical Application

Our interest in this conceptualization of the actor–event interface was aroused when we began to design our study of national policy domains, exploring the ways that actors participated in shaping specific policies over time. Once we successfully resolved the boundary-specification problem of identifying the set of consequential corporate actors in energy and health policy over the past 5–10 years, we were confronted with the task of specifying the set of events around which the actors' activities were organized. We defined an event as a critical, temporally ordered decision point in a collective decision-making sequence that must occur in order for a policy option to be authoritatively selected. Note that this definition involves two analytically separable dimensions—the institutional decision location and historical time—which provide the bases for formulating the principles of linkages among events.

Thus, two or more events may comprise distinct intermediate points in a chain of related decisions leading to an outcome. Obviously, chains of related decisions will be orchestrated differently, depending on the institutional arena in which the decision-making process takes place. Congressional passage of a bill involves a characteristic series of decision-points, such as House and Senate hearings, subcommittee and committee votes, and chamber actions, that follows a predictable, institutionally specified order differing in key respects from the process by which a federal agency comes to promulgate a new regulation. What is permissible for interested parties to do in one institutional arena may not be normatively approved in another because of different institutional rules. Thus, institutionalist theories of government functioning provide at least one significant basis for identifying key events to study and for anticipating the linkages among them.

The essence of the conceptual framework we propose for the analysis of policy decision making is a structural complex that connects consequential organizational actors with a set of temporally arrayed policy events. To understand how national policy unfolds, one must take into account how organizations perceive and respond to an opportunity structure for affecting policy outcomes that is created by the temporal sequence of policy-relevant events. Because a specific policy event is embedded in the context of other antecedent, concurrent, and impending events, policy analysts must incorporate the entire structure of organizations and events and not focus narrowly upon highly selected instances of either, as do most case studies (e.g., Dahl, 1961).

To be sure, multiple decision-making processes organized around diverse substantive issues claim the attentions of actors participating in a given policy domain. These diverse decision-making activities may be only loosely coupled with one another, if at all, and may proceed with time horizons of days, months, or years. Coupling of events may thus rest on an institutionally prescribed order or on widely shared, cross-cutting concern among the relevant actors about their outcomes.

In addition to the institutional scaffolding that links some events while segregating others, time itself is an ordering principle among events. Events do not occur in isolation but always are embedded in temporally ordered sequences, which shape the policy responses and initiatives of the core actors and set limits to the outcomes of collective decisions. Two fundamental aspects of time order are worth special mention. First, the mere fact that one event follows another establishes an incontrovertible and irreversible relationship between them that seemingly introduces an *inelectable dependence* of the second on the first that may have to be taken into account in the analysis. Conventional causal thinking is especially congenial with arguments stipulating that a subsequent event is an effect of (i.e., is causally dependent on) a prior event. But what about theories of strategic action that assert that a preferred end state outcome may "determine" how an actor participates in events leading up to that outcome (see Shepsle, 1979, for example). In this case, the causal order appears to be temporally reversed. Second, an event occurs by definition at a particular point in time that has a distinctive historicity shared with contemporaneous events but serving to distinguish them all from events occurring before and after that historical point. Debates about the desirability of establishing a national health insurance scheme, for example, had very different meanings for the participants in 1948, 1965, and 1980 (Starr, 1982). Similarly, during and immediately after the Arab oil embargo of 1973, events pertaining to energy policy attracted the attention of a far more diverse set of concerned parties and aroused quite different political dynamics from the times of abundant and cheap energy (McFarland, 1984).

Our argument does not claim such profound uniqueness for all events that it logically precludes their systematic analysis or comparison and confines us to narrative accounts of what happened. On the contrary, just as is regularly done for individual actors, we assume that events possess analytic features, such as controversiality, scope of impact, public visibility, and institutional locus, that impose empirical regularities on the political process and permit systematic comparisons. We may use these features in conceptualizing the structuration of events. The proximity of two events indicates that they are similar on the analytically relevant dimensions. One may then hypothesize that the closer the events, the higher the probability that similar actors will be attracted, and vice versa, the similarity of actors being defined by some relations based on the structural equivalence approach. This hypothesis would be a clear example of the kind of analysis that posits an interface between the structure of actors and the structure of events.

Let us illustrate the usefulness of the actor–event interface in explaining organizational participation in the policy domain with more specific examples. A naive predispositional framing perspective focuses on actors' individual characteristics (such as general interests and resources) in order to predict their activation by a set of events assumed to be statistically independent. To this model the concept of an actor–event interface adds a consideration of the characteristics of events that attract actors differentially. If one controls for actors' predispositional characteristics, certain events are shown to attract (or demand) particular types of actors. For example, highly visible events may attract different actors than publicly invisible events, even after controlling for organizational monitoring capacity and interests, because highly visible events themselves may entail an inherently different logic of participation (e.g., they may have different implications for strategic participation). Or events occurring at different institutional decision loci attract actors differentially to the extent that they have different implications for the legal mandate, institutional constraints, or institutional norms of the game.

How is the structure of events interfaced with the structure of actors in their policy participation? In responding to the puzzling question, "Why are there stable interorganizational relations?" network theorists argue persuasively that the stable relations exist because organizations strive to reduce uncertainty, information costs, and opportunistic behaviors of members by creating relatively stable channels of information inflow and thereby developing certain norms of the game (Leblebici and Salancik, 1982; Williamson, 1975, 1981, 1985). If the institutional norms are strong in a cooperative network, then a set of sequential events constituting distinct points in a chain of related decisions leading to an outcome will attract the actors who are embedded in the same structural locations in the network of actors. For example, members of a subdomain who have high communication density among themselves will be active throughout, from the first to the last event of the scenario. In short, structurally identical events recruit the participation of structurally identical actors, with a possible exception in the strategic participation of some powerful actors who can enjoy the margin of liberty (Crozier and Friedberg, 1980:45–63).

Comparison of several systems of action requires higher order concepts—what

Lazarsfeld and Menzel (1969) call global concepts—that characterize the organizational features of each system of action. For example, we have studied the energy and health policy domains as separate entities. One set of results suggests that the structure of communication linkages in the health domain is organized in a well-defined hierarchy, with centrally located actors who mediate communication among the peripherally located actors. In contrast, the energy domain has a more diffuse communication network lacking a coordinating set of actors; actors tend to be located on a wheel that puts them in close proximity with others sharing a narrowly defined concern and farther from every one else. We find interesting differences in the politics of the two domains as a result. Similarly, we study the structuration of the events in each domain. In the health domain, events appear to be sharply clustered on the basis of their specialized content and institutional loci for their decision making. Events attract narrowly defined constituencies, with little overlap across dissimilar events. In contrast, the energy policy domain processes events lacking much structural differentiation in terms of interested parties, content, or institutional loci of decision making. We conclude that the health domain in a given time frame is more institutionalized in its event structure than is the energy domain. Here we assert the testable proposition that the structuration of events in each domain has differing implications for the structuration of the social organization of the actors' participation in the domain.

Our approach enables us to analyze conflict and consensus over the resolution of policy issues in a domain. In light of the multitude of parties, both public and private, actively engaged in controversies over diverse policy issues, is it possible to specify principles that organize interested parties in a stable structure of cleavage and cooperation? Should not we expect, on the contrary, a fluid structure of almost random coalitions and oppositions for each contested event across the issue and event structures? Given a system of fluid coalitions, agreement or opposition between any pair of parties interested in a given event would depend solely on calculations of the marginal advantages and disadvantages of each policy option. Such calculations are unlikely to provide very consistent bases for ordering preferences across corporate actors, save, perhaps, for those whose organizational mandate is to be ideologically consistent even with respect to the most arcane "technical" questions.

Contrary to this view, however, we observe highly patterned structures of consensus and cleavage in the two domains. We have found a pattern of linkages among actors with respect to their policy interests, information exchanges, and involvement in institutionalized decision-making arenas.

The flow of candid and confidential information follows well-worn and enduring channels among mutually trusted actors sharing common interests and broadly similar postures toward issues of importance to them. That is, actors regularly turn to trusted others for interpretive and strategic information concerning "what is going on" and "what is to be done." Timely information gained from these confidential exchanges helps to orchestrate the individual actors' strategic policy interventions. The pattern of confidential exchanges in a given policy domain constitutes the *enduring* structure or scaffolding in which all the actors are embedded and, as a result, granted easy or limited access to relevant information on topics of interest to them. Analogously, we might speak of such a structure as a crystal that is left intact or subjected to breakage along different fault lines, depending on the blows it receives from various policy-relevant events.

To pursue the analogy, and to further illustrate our approach, Figures 2.2 and 2.3 indicate the sets of supporters and opponents activated in three hotly contested scenarios in each policy domain. The actors' locations in each figure coincide with their positions in confidential communication networks in energy and health. The contiguity curve drawn in each insert attempts to segregate the proponents (indicated by squares) from the opponents (indicated by circles). "Errors" occur when one observes opponents on the supporters' side of the curve, or vice versa. What is remarkable is how clearly delineated the supporter and opponent sectors are in each contested matter. Yet the patterns of cleavage shift dramatically from event scenario to scenario as the symbolic content changes. Also noteworthy is the fact that the contiguity curve always traverses the center box containing the actors most active in the communication network (who are also among the most influential actors). Note that the curve divides actors in the central box into opposing sides, reflecting the active role these peak organizations play in mediating the conflict as they place opposing parties in relatively close communicative proximity to one another. In general, the farther from the center of the space along some axis, the more completely the sector is dominated by either opponents or supporters of a particular outcome.

Returning to the analogy of breaking a crystal, we know that given the structure of the crystal, how it splits depends on the strength and precise incidence of the chisel blow. Similarly, much of the strategic action of event participants, including even the matter of who decides to participate and on what side, concerns the negotiation of how the issue will be framed so that it selectively energizes the interests and actions of certain domain members in behalf of particular outcomes and discourages others from entering the deliberations. A consensual chorus results when the generally accepted frame successfully neutralizes the mobilization of potential opponents by stressing the facilitative, nonadversarial character of the policy question.

In the energy domain, the three inserts in Figure 2.2 describe partisan participation in three nuclear energy events (Clinch River nuclear breeder reactor funding, nuclear waste storage plans, and the nuclear power plant construction moratorium). The correlation of participants' positions are quite high across these three events (from $r = .50$ to $.92$), reflecting the consistency with which

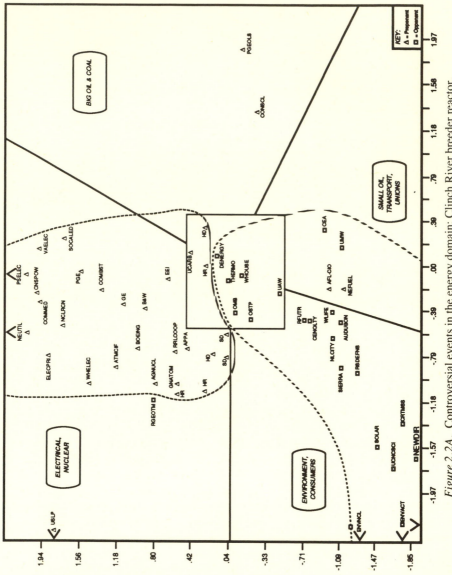

Figure 2.2A. Controversial events in the energy domain: Clinch River breeder reactor.

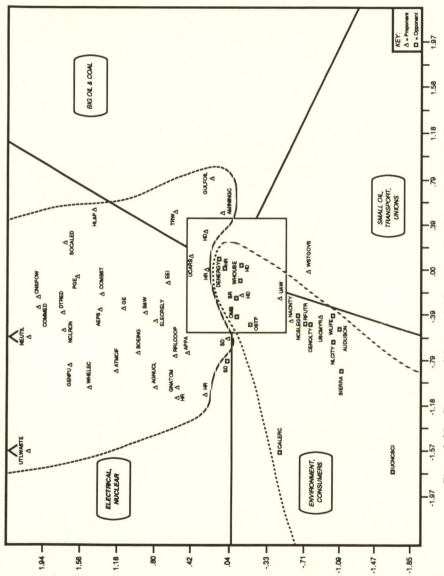

Figure 2.2B. Controversial events in the energy domain: nuclear waste disposal.

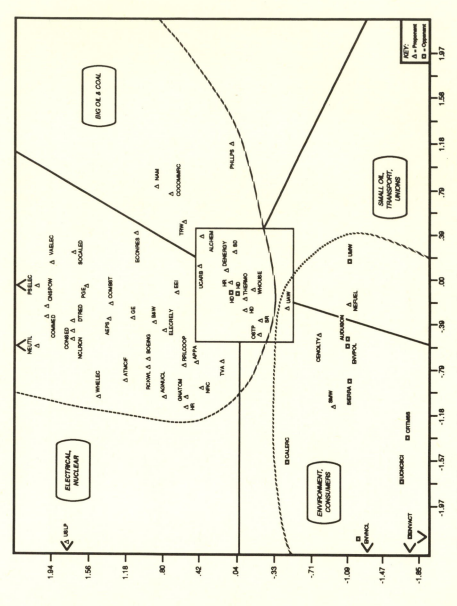

Figure 2.2C. Controversial events in the energy domain: moratorium on nuclear plant construction.

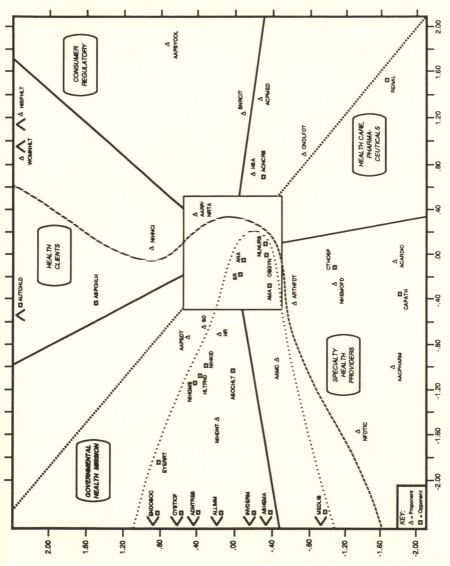

Figure 2.3A. Controversial events in the health domain: control of funding for the NIH.

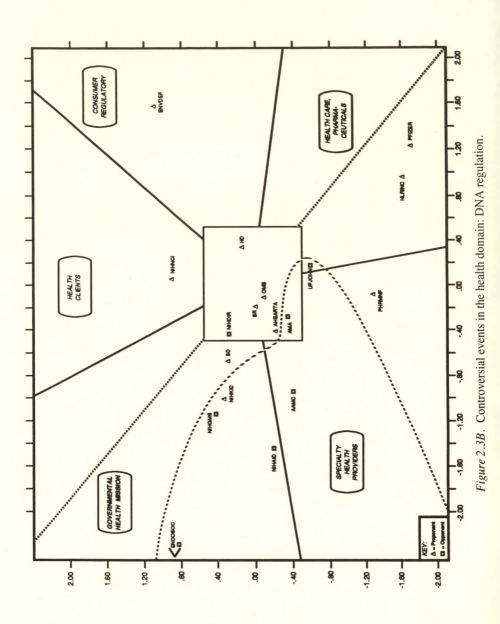

Figure 2.3B. Controversial events in the health domain: DNA regulation.

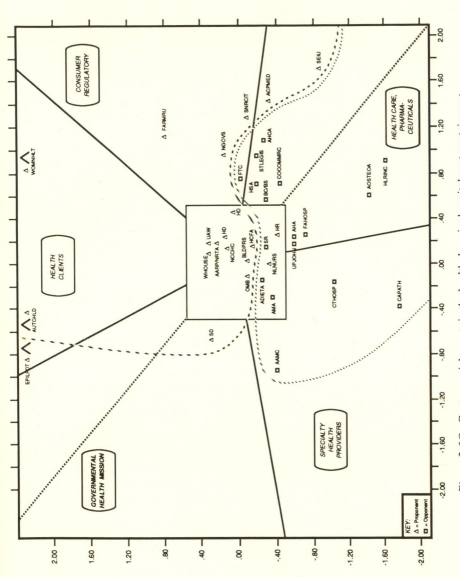

Figure 2.3C. Controversial events in the health domain: hospital cost containment.

41

the environmentalist groups in the lower lefthand region challenged the manufac-
turers of nuclear equipment and the public utilities with heavy nuclear investments, which were concentrated in the upper center and upper right portions of
the confidential communication space. The proenvironmental coalition penetrated
deeply into the core region on these three events, receiving aggressive support
from key government actors in the White House, Energy Department, and Office
of Management and Budget (OMB). Only on the nuclear plant moratorium
question, following the Three Mile Island accident, did the antinuclear forces fail
to garner support from central government actors. The key sponsors of the
amendment were lodged within a House subcommittee, but the full House
decisively defeated the proposal in a vote that occurred after the Nuclear
Regulatory Commission had already decided not to issue new permits until the
Three Mile Island accident was fully investigated. The three events show that a
nuclear energy subdomain had clearly coalesced into a bipolar opposition
structure. The two coalitions—augmented or decremented from event to event by
interested actors that entered or left in response to distinctive features of
particular events—squared off in a rancorous fight over the future of the
American nuclear industry. By the end of the decade, a convergence of safety,
cost, and environmental issues had torn apart the cozy triangle among private
capital, the Atomic Energy Commission, and congressional oversight committees
of the 1950s and 1960s that had once promised electricity "too cheap to meter."
A number of other prominent energy controversies explored in Laumann and
Knoke (1987: Chapter 12), including the fights over windfall profits and gas
deregulation, are almost wholly incoherent in the patterning of actors' participation and preferences when compared to the more tightly interrelated controversies
over nuclear energy matters described in Figure 2.2.

Turning to the health domain (Figure 2.3), we observe that the first two inserts
refer to issues related to funding biomedical research or biomedically linked
regulatory matters. Supporters and opponents are selectively activated in the
broad regions of the space populated with actors whose mandates are especially
concerned with such matters. Each scenario elicited a distinctive set of
participants with relatively limited overlap with participants in what would
generally appear to be substantively relates scenarios. Insert 3 (referring to the
cost containment issue, one of the premier controversies of the period) arrays the
hospital establishment against government and lay actors concerned with paying
for rapidly rising hospital charges.

A superb instance of the process of frame negotiation is found in the great cost
containment controversy of 1977 (Figure 2.3) in which President Carter through
the White House Office and OMB, together with his Democratic allies in the
relevant House and Senate subcommittees, proposed mandatory cost caps on
hospital charges. The strategy was to single out hospital charges in an effort to
control the rising level of government expenditures on health care and, perhaps,

in hopes of driving a wedge into the ranks of the medical establishment. The American Hospital Association (AHA), with its allies in various sectors of the hospital industry, the drug industry, and even the American Medical Association (AMA) (which did not have a direct stake, since doctors' charges would not be subject to this control, but which was ideologically opposed to increased governmental regulation) counterattacked with a proposal for voluntary price control by the hospitals themselves. Note that none of the specialty doctors' professional associations actively opposed the Carter proposal except for the pathologists, an almost exclusively hospital-based group. Given the rapidly increasing cost of employee medical insurance premiums, the financial interests of many members of the U.S. Chamber of Commerce might have been better served by a mandatory cap, but it nevertheless supported the AHA initiative, presumably on the basis of ideological opposition to government-imposed price regulation. Blue Cross/Blue Shield was originally founded by the AHA and AMA and subsequently enjoyed close ties with them, perpetuated by overlapping boards of directors and frequent exchanges of personnel. It actively supported the AHA's position, but the association of private (for profit) health insurers remained inactive. The latter were, to say the least, ambivalent on the issue because of conflicting ideological and financial considerations. One suspects that Blue Cross/Blue Shield was subjected to cross-pressures that were resolved in favor of voluntary cost containment because of its special relation to the AHA.

Only some of the unions most closely allied with Carter supported his initiative; the AFL/CIO ànd the United Mine Workers (UMW) were silent, since their party loyalties and general interest in curtailing rising costs were offset by the concern that cost containment legislation might threaten the wages of health care workers. In fact, the coalition supporting mandatory control was drawn from the Democratic side of the congressional subcommittees, executive agencies, such as Health Care Financing Administration (HCFA) and OMB, confronted with escalating hospital charges in the Medicare and Medicaid budgets, the associations of state and local government officials responsible for providing health care to citizens on welfare and public assistance, and various associations of senior citizens especially concerned with maintaining the financial viability, while expanding the coverage, of the Medicare program. As the debate over Carter's hospital cost containment plan extended through the next 2 years, support for the plan was severely eroded. Increasingly aware that it was a partial, and extremely cumbersome, response to the rising cost of health care, a number of congressional Democrats threw their support to the voluntary plan proposed by the hospital industry. Others, led by Senator Edward Kennedy, became more zealous in insisting on a system of national health insurance as the only equitable and effective method of controlling costs and, consequently, the level of government expenditures.

The principal conclusion of this analysis is the remarkable orderliness in the patterning of consensus and cleavage in the two policy domains. It is not, however, an orderliness easily comprehended by one or two broad analytic distinctions that refer simply to pervasive ideological disagreements among the actors or to master corporate identities with known and unchanging interests. This order is best thought of as a multidimensional structuring of distinctions among interested parties that are selectively activated during the ongoing discourse on what is to be done in a sequence of events. Each actor possesses an array of corporate interests, resources, and linkages with others—that is, strategic considerations—that embeds it in a multidimensional structure of commitments selectively activated by features of the events being processed in an interactive fashion to which each actor contributes and responds. To study such structures more effectively, we must devise more sophisticated methods for analyzing the multidimensionally organized interface of events and actors that preserve its global character.

Concluding Overview of Results

Throughout our analyses, we were impressed by the degree of convergence across the energy and health domains. We began with a presumption that health would be more institutionalized and energy more fluid. And, in fact, our analyses consistently explained more variance—with respect to both organizational behavior and event outcomes—in the data that were gathered for the health domain. Although the differences that emerged lay in the expected direction, the similarities in structures and processes are too striking to ignore. Hence, in this summary we emphasize common relationships across the domains.

The core populations of national policy domains consist of large numbers of private as well as public organizations. About three-quarters of the hundreds of key actors are nongovernmental collectivities. Their presence in large numbers reveals the limitations of policymaking studies that focus exclusively upon the microprocesses of influence within governmental institutions such as Congress and the executive agencies. Despite their lack of formal decision-making authority, many private participants possess sufficient political clout to ensure that their expressed interests will be taken into account by other actors. This mutual recognition creates and sustains the legitimacy of core actors' involvement in domain issues and events. We did not gather data on the thousands of claimant groups that exist outside the inner core, but we believe that the core private and public sector organizations rarely acknowledge these bit-players as meaningful actors within the policymaking process. Their salience is too low and their costs of entry are too high to secure more than episodic and grudging acknowledgment of their existence by the core actors. In explaining most decisions, the peripheral organizations may be ignored, although their omission may carry negative connotations for normative democratic theory.

Within the group of core participants, however, there exists a relatively dense system of interorganizational interaction. Our analyses of patterns of communication among a highly diverse set of organizations revealed a considerable level of connectedness. For routine communication, the ratio of actual ties to potential ties was .30 in both domains; for confidential communication, the ratio decreased to .19 in the energy domain and .17 in health. None of the actors is isolated, and all are mutually reachable within three steps. These results are comparable to those reported by studies of communication density within far more homogeneous or functionally interdependent sets of organizations than the group interviewed for this project. And these networks of communication serve to orchestrate participation with respect to domain events in ways that remain undetected in analyses restricted to the relationships between the attributes of individual organizations and their political activity.

To specify a large and tightly interconnected set of domain core actors is not to assert that each possesses identical power and influence within the domain. Indeed, there are large variations in size and wealth between organizational types as well as within each of these categories. Yet we did not discover strong relationships between resources and overall reputation. Although influence rank is predicted to some degree by "hard" resource holdings (such as money, employees, and public authority) and "soft" resources (such as impartial mediation and public mobilization), the vast majority of core actors within these domains possess sufficient resources to render purely quantitative assessments irrelevant for understanding policy behavior. In fact, one of the resources commonly associated with participation in the making of policy in the theoretical literature—the size of staffs available to monitor ongoing domain activities —proved unrelated to participation in policy events.

Despite the relative absence of a direct relationship between participation and individual organizational attributes, within each domain we uncovered a number of highly differentiated social structures that order the core organizations into central and peripheral positions. One of the most unequal hierarchies is influence–reputation ranking. The highest-ranking organizations tend to be governmental actors, generalist trade associations and professional societies, and major corporations. At the bottom are found specialist associations, public interest groups, and similar claimant organizations having either narrow or incidental interests in the domain. An organization's reputation is an amalgam of its past successful influence, present strategic location, and future (anticipated) exploits, with a little misperception thrown in. Within the health domain, however, there was a high degree of consensus on these points. In the energy domain, by contrast, there was a marked bifurcation in the perceptions of organizations' relative standing within the policy arena. Consumer and environmental groups tended to see executive agencies as the most authoritative, whereas business organizations attributed greater influence to trade associations as well as to Congress. We found little evidence that the character of political activity varied systematically among different sorts of organizations, thereby producing the patterns of executive and congressional specialization that have been noted in some studies.

In addition to stratification in terms of attributed influence, both energy and health domains are also highly differentiated along lines of policy interest. No organizations, even generalist government actors mandated to scrutinize and coordinate domain affairs, distributed their attention so as to occupy a central location in the issue space. Instead, issue publics are arrayed like beads on a bracelet. Typically, an organization's substantive goals determine the cluster of issues on which it concentrates its time and effort. Thus, coal companies ignore nuclear power, solar energy, and oil import fees. The norm of fighting for one's own interests but not against another's serves to reinforce a narrow vision of proper partisan conduct for most organizations. Even the environmental interests groups—which perceive dangers in many types of fuel usage—are highly selective in their attention to issues, in large measure because of the need to husband their resources. The result is a substantially balkanized domain structure, with a dozen or more subdomains in which most of the core organizations invest their resources. In the absence of a central subset of actors with diversified issue portfolios, the domain structure is better characterized as elite interest group pluralism rather than centralized coordination.

When we turn to the structure of confidential communication within policy domains, however, a core/periphery structure is clearly visible. This system of organization simultaneously reflects levels of participation and influence as well as differentiated concerns and policy preferences. Information exchanges in national policy domains are instrumentally structured at both micro (dyadic) and global (whole system) levels. Organizations generate and sustain ties to one another because of substantive similarities in their issue and event interests. Communication partners are instrumental collective actors, either as potential supporters and opponents or as targets of influence efforts.

The major governmental actors—the White House, OMB, cabinet departments, key House and Senate subcommittees—occupy the center of the communication network. As formal authorities, they are targets of numerous information and influence communications. Arrayed around this core subset are the generalist trade associations, professional societies, and major corporations. They seem to mediate communication between the central authorities and the peripheral specialist actors that occupy the remoter subregions of the communication space. These specialists may be recruited by the generalists to form temporary coalitions or action sets (see Knoke and Burleigh, 1988) in pursuit of specific, limited objectives. In the fight over cost containment, hospital trade associations mobilized selected groups of medical professionals, notably the hospital-based pathologists, while the major physicians' societies, though sympathetic, remained on the sidelines. Similarly, in the incident that opened this chapter, a decision by the FAA unintentionally generated a working alliance among firms that, typically separated by fuel-specific concerns, shared a set of specialized concerns associated with exploration for new reserves. Thus, the highly differentiated communication networks, in conjunction with the issue interests of the actors, define the constraints within which subsequent policy fights are conducted.

Organizational activation on a specific event is a joint function of the event's characteristics (especially visibility, scope, and controversiality) and the organization's own attributes (particularly its interest in the underlying issues and its location in the communication network). At the same time, neither organizations nor events "possess" attributes in some absolute sense but take on meanings by becoming embedded in a system of organizational action and interaction through the recognition of events and the construction of scenarios. Thus, collective efforts to influence the outcome of public policy events involve both micro-level (actor-based) and global (system-level) social forces. Because of the interpenetrating nature of these processes, we cannot assign causal priority to either dynamic, nor indeed is this necessarily an appropriate goal for all theory construction. One way to visualize this dialectic is to imagine a carpet into which a figure is woven in a contrasting color. When attention focuses on the figure, the background threads recede in salience. Yet one need only flip the carpet over to appreciate that the figure is defined by, and inseparable from, the context upon which it is arranged. Likewise, every event–organization configuration is created by the simultaneous intersection of historical opportunity with actor dispositions: trying to explicate one without the other is folly.

When participation in individual events is aggregated for an organization, the level of its activity within the domain is clearly a function of its scope of interest, interorganizational resource exchanges, and influence reputation, but not its location in the communication network or its monitoring capacity (see Laumann, Knoke, and Kim, 1985). Obviously, activation depends upon certain stable structural properties of the organizations embedded in the policy domain, as well as upon idiosyncratic attributes not investigated in our project. However, in collapsing an organization's activity level across all possible events, to some extent we create an analytic artifact. That is, events actually occur in a temporally distributed succession rather than simultaneously. Characterizing each organization only according to the number of events in which it was publicly active violates this historically contingent process of mobilization. Thus, although we now understand some of the individual- and system-level forces related to domain organizations' participation in policy events, much more work remains to be done on how the timing and sequence of events interacts with actors' attributes to mobilize domain activity.

Explaining the outcome of policy events is the ultimate focus of our research. From our perspective on the emerging organizational state, one must never neglect the fact that many—indeed, most—decision-making events, even one of considerable consequence, are worked on by only a limited number of actors, and by the endstage of the decision-making process, there is little, if any, controversy about the policy option that will be implemented. Decisions typically pass into the structure of constraints unremarked, but not, therefore, without considerable consequences for future policy. Indeed, one very important type of event is defined as recurrent and noncontroversial. Participants in these decision processes are usually recruited from a narrow region of the policy domains, and the mode of decision making is expert and technocratic. In fact, only a very limited number of matters are selected for dispute and public controversy, the result of poorly understood processes whereby key actors come to contest the symbolic framing in which "routine" decisions heretofore had been made.

By limiting the number and range of actors recognized as knowledgeable and legitimate participants, these "routine" understandings of the nature of policy events help to stabilize the organization of policy domains. In addition, however, we selected for detailed analysis eight highly controversial events, spanning diverse issue areas, in each domain. Each event attracted unique constellations of openly partisan organizations. The typical cleavage patterns bifurcate the communication structure: one group of actors favoring the outcome of the policy proposal and a second subset of opponents. Most significantly, these opposition groups form idiosyncratic coalitions across substantively different events. Yet, somewhat paradoxically, it is possible to acknowledge widely varying patterns of organizational participation without abandoning the assumption that some sort of relatively stable social structure nevertheless orders much activity. Social order is not limited to the regular association of specific traits with particular behaviors.

Finally, we developed exchange models, first proposed by Coleman (1973), and applied them to selected controversial issues in each domain. Despite the level of attention directed toward the collective structure of these two policy domains, the fact that organizations are, at least potentially, autonomous and strategic actors should not be forgotten. Two models of organizational interaction were developed to identify what types of strategic action are of greatest consequence. The operative factors in the resource deployment and resource mobilization models are the domain organization's interests in each event and their relative control over the outcomes of these events through resource exchanges. Assuming the achievement of equilibrium after exchanging resources, tests of the models' effectiveness proved highly accurate in predicting both the organization's power over events and the domain's collective outcomes for every event. Business organizations in energy and professional societies in health proved most influential for collective decisions. The resource deployment and mobilization models jointly identified resource exchanges between pairs of organizations. Interestingly, the interaction term accounted for the greatest part of the variance of resource transactions. Beyond this, however, we discovered that resource mobilization strategy within the private sector was more important than the resource mobilization strategy of government organizations in explaining the resource flow from the private to the public sector.

In conclusion, our research on the social organization of the U.S. national energy and health domains indicates the existence of large, exclusive, highly differentiated communities of policy-making organizations. According to narrowly specified issue agendas, they pursue events through the communication of intent, the mobilization of support, and the targeting of influence efforts. Resource exchanges lie at the heart of the influence system and account for the process of collective decision. Overall, policies are the product of decentralized contention among a plurality of organizations seeking to satisfy their interests by influencing public authorities.

Conclusion

This chapter examines collective action in the organizational state. It investigates the structuration of policy events and organizations in the American energy and health national policy domains. The result is a deeper understanding of how the political economy of the modern organizational state operates.

Two decades ago, Grant McConnell (1969:155) observed that:

> In the United States, at least, private associations have also contributed to order and stability through a pattern of relationships with government to a degree which is seldom acknowledged. In a multitude of ways, the distinction between what is private and what is public has been blurred so that it is often extraordinarily difficult to determine what is the character of a particular form of action or rule.

This interlacing of public and private sectors has not gone so far in America as in some Western European nations characterized by corporatist polities (Panitch, 1977; Schmitter, 1981). In Austria, Scandinavia, and other nations with strong labor movements and socialist parties, governmental authority has devolved to a set of intermediary ("peak") associations of employers and workers. The state authorizes and consults with them in negotiating, regulating, and implementing policies that affect their members, for example, in setting wages and prices, production and labor conditions, occupational qualifications and training, and welfare provisions (Williamson, 1985:78–79). Although for historical reasons, the devolution of state power was more limited in the United States (Salisbury, 1984; Wilson, 1982), the blurred boundaries noted two decades ago by McConnell have grown even fuzzier. State bureaucracies' strategies vis-à-vis civil society emerged from basic organizational imperatives for coping with environmental uncertainties, resource scarcities, and sociolegal constraints

(Knoke and Burleigh, 1988). In their efforts to maximize autonomy, state bureaus fostered stable networks of clientele, funding sources, and interorganizational alliances:

> The successful agencies expand, garnering more projects and larger budgets under their control. In this process of increasing the predictability of their specific environment, public bureaucracies incorporate external constituencies, blurring the boundary line between public and private sectors, as they establish powerful interest groups inside and outside the state with a stake in the preservation of the agency (Alford and Friedland, 1985:436).

The historical creation of the liberal democratic state was accompanied by a parallel transformation of social segments into organized interest groups with claims on access to the new centers of social power (McNeil, 1978). Interdependency and reciprocated relations between state bureaus and private associations jointly created the modern organizational state. Neither a structure for capitalist class rule nor a neutral umpire adjudicating claims of competing groups, the state is a system of governmental and nongovernmental organizations that struggle for power and legitimacy in the making of public policies. Rather than reflecting rigid ideological stances, the policy objectives sought by these participants reflect organizational imperatives for profits, growth, market share, jurisdiction, autonomy, and similarly narrow and pragmatic concerns. The result is that cleavages within policy domains display the idiosyncratic nature of shifting organizational interests, rather than rigid inflexible alignments structured along class, industry, or party dimensions. Most collective policy decisions involve shifting interorganizational coalitions and influence interactions. Cooperation among organizations that share a common preference for an event outcome raises the probability that their efforts will produce a favorable decision. Coalitions of organizations pool resources and coordinate their common efforts to overcome their opponents and persuade the public authorities of the merits of their case. Such processes of contention among opposing interest group coalitions, including partisan governmental organizations, are the key dynamic for any understanding of collective decision making in national policy domains.

Notes

1. Numerous studies of local community politics focus on natural persons as key actors in community decision making (e.g., Hunter, 1953; Laumann and Pappi, 1976). When we speak of someone playing a decision-making or leadership role as a natural person, we mean to imply that he or she is acting primarily in behalf of his/her unique bundle of personal and social identities and not as a fiduciary agent of a corporate (or organizational) actor. We believe that

natural persons themselves are playing less significant roles in national-level politics, even though we do not entirely ignore their importance (cf. Coleman, 1974; 1982).

2. More concretely, we operationally define national health policies to be concerned with: the provision and distribution of medical (including dental) services, pharmaceuticals, and medical devices; prevention and containment of contagion or disease; and screening of food additives, drugs, and medical treatments or procedures for potential hazards. Specifically included within this domain are policies concerned with mental health; the regulation of doctors, dentists, medical technicians, hospital administrators, and other health care providers; the training and certification of such health care providers; the regulation of hospitals, clinics, and other institutions that provide medical services; the regulation of the manufacture and distribution of drugs and medical devices; the financing of providers of health care and the regulation of both public and private health insurance; and the special health problems of identifiable subgroups of the population, including veterans, Native Americans, and the elderly. Specifically excluded from the domain are policies concerned with access of handicapped persons and occupational safety issues (OSHA).

With respect to energy, we include policies concerned with: the production, distribution, consumption, and externalities imposed by the use of fuels for the generation of heat, light, or motive power, whether for ultimate consumption in industrial, commercial, institutional, or residential settings. The fuels include oil, natural gas, manufactured gas (propane), other petroleum by-products, alcohol, coal, electricity (whether generated by fossil fuel, nuclear fission and fusion, water, or other means), synthetic fuels, biomass, geothermal, wind, water, and solar energy (see Heinz *et al.,* 1982: Appendix I).

References

Alba, Richard D., and Moore, Gwen (1978). "Elite social circles." *Sociological Methods and Research* 7:167–188.

Aldrich, Howard E. (1979). *Organizations and Environments.* Englewood Cliffs, N.J.: Prentice-Hall.

Aldrich, Howard E., and Pfeffer, Jeffrey (1976). "Environments and organizations." *Annual Review of Sociology* 2:79–105.

Alford, Robert P., and Friedland, Roger (1985). *Powers of Theory: Capitalism, the State, and Democracy.* Cambridge: Cambridge University Press.

Allison, Graham T. (1971). *Essence of Decision: Explaining the Cuban Missile Crisis.* Boston: Little, Brown.

Barton, Allen H. (1975). "Consensus and conflict among American leaders." *Public Opinion Quarterly* 38:507–530.

Benson, J. Kenneth (1975). "The interorganizational network as political economy." *Administrative Science Quarterly* 20:229–249.

Berry, Jeffrey M. (1984). *The Interest Group Society*. Boston: Little, Brown.

Billings, Robert S., Milburn, Thomas W., and Schaalman, Mary Lou (1980). "A model of crisis perception: A theoretical and empirical analysis." *Administrative Science Quarterly* 25:300–316.

Block, Fred (1977). "The ruling class does not rule: Notes on the Marxist theory of the state." *Socialist Revolution* 7:6–28.

Boorman, Scott A., and White, Harrison C. (1976). "Social structure from multiple networks, II: Role structure." *American Journal of Sociology* 81:1384–1446.

Burstein, Paul (1981). "The sociology of democratic politics and government." *Annual Review of Sociology* 7:291–319.

Burt, Ronald S. (1976). "Positions in networks." *Social Forces* 55:93–122.

Burt, Ronald S. (1977). "Power as a social typology." *Social Science Research* 6:1–83.

Burt, Ronald S. (1978). "Cohesion versus structural equivalence as a basis for network subgroups." *Sociological Methods and Research* 7:189–212.

Burton, Michael G., and Higley, John (1984). "Elite theory: The basic contentions." Paper presented at the annual meetings of the American Sociological Association, San Antonio, Texas.

Cobb, Roger W., and Elder, Charles D. (1972). *Participation in American Politics: The Dynamics of Agenda-Building*. Baltimore: Johns Hopkins University Press.

Coleman, James S. (1973). *The Mathematics of Collective Action*. Chicago: Aldine.

Coleman, James S. (1974). *Power and the Structure of Society*. New York: W.W. Norton.

Coleman, James S. (1982). *The Asymmetric Society*. Syracuse, N.Y.: Syracuse University Press.

Cook, Karen S. (1977). "Exchange and power in networks in interorganizational relations." *Sociological Quarterly* 18:62–82.

Crozier, Michel, and Friedberg, Erhard (1980). *Actors and Systems: The Politics of Collective Action*. Translated by Arthur Goldhammer. Chicago: University of Chicago Press.

Dahl, Robert A. (1961). *Who Governs? Democracy and Power in an American City*. New Haven: Yale University Press.

Domhoff, G. William (1978). *The Powers That Be: Process of Ruling-Class Domination of America*. New York: Vintage Books.

Dye, Thomas R. (1976). *Who's Running America?* Englewood Cliffs, N.J.: Prentice-Hall.

Field, G. Lowell, and Higley, John (1980). *Elitism*. London: Routledge and Kegan Paul.

Gais, Thomas L., Peterson, Mark A., and Walker, Jack L. (1984). "Interest groups, iron triangles, and representative institutions in American national government." *British Journal of Political Science* 14:161–181.

Galaskiewicz, Joseph (1979). *Exchange Networks and Community Politics*. Beverly Hills, Calif.: Sage Publications.

Gamson, William A. (1975). *The Strategy of Social Protest*. Homewood, Ill.: Dorsey Press.

Garson, G. David (1978). *Group Theories of Politics*. Beverly Hills, Calif.: Sage.

Gold, David, Lo, Clarence, and Wright, Erik Olin (1975). "Recent developments in Marxist theories of the capitalist state." *Monthly Review* 27:29–41.

Granovetter, Mark S. (1985). "Economic action, social structure, and embeddedness." *American Journal of Sociology* 91:481–510.

Griffin, Larry J., Devine, Joel A., and Wallace, Michael (1982). "Monopoly capital, organized labor, and military expenditures in the United States, 1949–1976." *American Journal of Sociology Suppl.* 88:113–153.

Hayes, Michael T. (1979). "Interest groups and Congress: Toward a transactional theory." In Leroy N. Rieselbach (ed.), *The Congressional System,* 2d ed. North Scituate, Mass.: Duxbury, pp. 252–273.

Heinz, John P., and Laumann, Edward O. (1982). *Chicago Lawyers: The Social Structure of the Bar.* New York: Russell Sage Foundation, American Bar Foundation.

Heinz, John P., Laumann, Edward O., Nelson, Robert, and Salisbury, Robert (1982). "Washington representatives and national policy making." A proposal to the Trustees of the American Bar Foundation. New York: American Bar Foundation.

Hermann, Charles F. (1969). *Crisis in Foreign Policy: A Simulation Analysis.* Indianapolis, Ind.: Bobbs-Merrill.

Hicks, Alexander, and Swank, Duane (1984). "On the political economy of welfare expansion: A comparative analysis of 18 advanced capitalist democracies, 1960–1971." *Comparative Political Studies* 17:81–119.

Hunter, Floyd (1953). *Community Power Structure.* Durham: University of North Carolina Press.

Jacobs, David (1974). "Dependency and vulnerability: An exchange approach to the control of organizations." *Administrative Science Quarterly* 19:45–59.

Kingdon, John W. (1984). *Agendas, Alternatives, and Public Policies.* Boston: Little, Brown.

Knoke, David (1981). "Power structures." In Samuel L. Long (ed.), *The Handbook of Political Behavior,* Vol. 3. New York: Plenum, pp. 275–332.

Knoke, David, and Burleigh, Frank (1988). "Collective Action in National Policy Domains: Constraints, Cleavages and Policy Outcomes." *Research in Political Sociology* 4:forthcoming.

Knoke, David, and Laumann, Edward O. (1982). "The social organization of national policy domains: An exploration of some structural hypotheses." In Peter V. Marsden and Nan Lin (eds.), *Social Structure and Network Analysis.* Beverly Hills, Calif.: Sage Publications, pp. 255–270.

Laumann, Edward O., and Heinz, John P. (1985). "Washington lawyers—and others: The structure of Washington representation." *Stanford Law Review* 37:465–502.

Laumann, Edward O., and Knoke, David (1987). *The Organizational State: Social Choice in National Policy Domains.* Madison: University of Wisconsin Press.

Laumann, Edward O., and Marsden, Peter V. (1982). "Microstructural analysis in interorganizational systems." *Social Networks* 4:329–348.

Laumann, Edward O., and Pappi, Franz U. (1976). *Networks of Collective Action: A Perspective on Community Influence Systems.* New York: Academic.

Laumann, Edward O., Galaskiewicz, Joseph, and Marsden, Peter V. (1978). "Community structure as interorganizational linkages." *Annual Review or Sociology* 4:455–484.

Laumann, Edward O., Knoke, David, and Kim, Yong-Hak (1985). "An organizational approach to state policy formation: A comparative study of energy and health domains." *American Sociological Review* 50:1–19.

Lazarsfeld, Paul F., and Menzel, Herbert (1969). "On the relation between individual and collective properties." In Amitai Etzioni (ed.), *A Sociological Reader on Complex Organizations*, 2d ed. New York: Holt, Reinhart and Winston, pp. 499–516.

Leblebici, Huseyin, and Salancik, Gerald (1982). "Stability in interorganizational exchange: Rulemaking processes of the Chicago Board of Trade." *Administrative Science Quarterly* 27:227–242.

Lyles, Marjorie A., and Mitroff, Ian I. (1980). "Organizational problem formulation: An empirical study." *Administrative Science Quarterly* 25:102–119.

McConnell, Grant (1966). *Private Power and American Democracy*. New York: Knopf.

McConnell, Grant (1969). "The public values of the private association." In J. Roland Pennock and John W. Chapman (eds.), *Voluntary Associations*. New York: Atherton Press, pp. 147–160.

McFarland, Andrew S. (1983). "Public interest lobbies versus minority faction." In Allan J. Cigler and Burdett A. Loomis (eds.), *Interest Group Politics*. Washington, D.C.: CQ Press, pp. 324–353.

McNeil, Kenneth (1978). "Understanding organizational power: Building on the Weberian legacy." *Administrative Science Quarterly* 23:65–90.

March, James G., and Olsen, Johan P. (1976). *Ambiguity and Choice in Organizations*. Bergen: Universitetsforlaget.

Marsden, Peter V., and Laumann, Edward O. (1977). "Collective action in a community elite: Exchange, influence resources, and issue resolution." In R.J. Liebert and A.W. Imershein (eds.), *Power, Paradigms, and Community Research*. London: Sage, pp. 199–250.

Miliband, Ralph (1969). *The State in Capitalist Society*. London: Merlin Press.

Mills, C. Wright (1956). *The Power Elite*. New York: Oxford University Press.

Moore, Gwen (1979). "The structure of a national elite network." *American Sociological Review* 44:673–691.

Nelson, Robert, Heinz, John P., Laumann, Edward O., and Salisbury, Robert (1987). "Interest representation in Washington: Lawyers, lobbyists and more." *American Bar Foundation Research Journal*, in press.

Offe, Claus, and Ronge, Volker (1975). "Theses on the theory of the state." *New German Critique* 6:137–147.

Panitch, Leon (1977). "The development of corporatism in liberal democracies." *Comparative Political Studies* 10:61–90.

Parsons, Talcott (1951). *The Social System*. Glencoe, Ill.: Free Press.

Parsons, Talcott (1969). *Politics and Social Structure*. New York: Free Press.

Perrucci, R., and Pilisuk, Mark (1970). "Leaders and ruling elites: The interorganizational bases of community power." *American Sociological Review* 35:1040–1057.

Poulantzas, Nicos (1973). *Political Power and Social Classes*. London: New Left Books.

Ripley, Randall B., and Franklin, Grace A. (1980). *Congress, the Bureaucracy, and Public Policy*. Revised ed. Homewood, Ill.: Dorsey Press.

Sailer, Lee D. (1978). "Structural equivalence: Meaning and definition, computation and application." *Social Networks* 1:73–90.

Salisbury, Robert H. (1984). "Interest representation: The dominance of institutions." *American Political Science Review* 78:64–76.

Schlozman, Kay L., and Tierney, John T. (1983). "More of the same: Washington pressure group activity in a decade of change." *Journal of Politics* 34:351–377.

Schmitter, Phillipe C. (1979). "Still the century of corporatism?" In Phillipe C. Schmitter and Gerhard Lehmbruch (eds.), *Trends toward Corporatist Intermediation*. Beverly Hills, Calif.: Sage Publications, pp. 7–52.

Schmitter, Phillipe C. (1981). "Interest intermediation and regime governability in contemporary western Europe and North America." In Suzanne D. Berger, ed., *Organizing Interests in Western Europe*. Cambridge: Cambridge University Press, pp. 287–330.

Scott, Richard W. (1981). *Organizations: Rational, Natural and Open Systems*. Englewood Cliffs, N.J.: Prentice-Hall.

Shepsle, Kenneth A. (1979). "Institutional arrangements and equilibrium in multidimensional voting models." *American Journal of Political Science* 23:27–59.

Skocpol, Theda (1979). *States and Social Revolutions*. New York: Cambridge University Press.

Skocpol, Theda (1980). "Political response to capitalist crisis: Neo-Marxist theories of the state and the case of the New Deal." *Politics and Society* 10:155–201.

Smelser, Neil (1962). *Theory of Collective Behavior*. New York: Free Press.

Starr, Paul (1982). *The Social Transformation of American Medicine: The Rise of a Sovereign Profession and the Making of a Vast Industry*. New York: Basic Books.

Therborn, Goran (1976). "What does the ruling class do when it rules?" *Insurgent Sociologist* 6:3–16.

Tilly, Charles (1978). *From Mobilization to Revolution*. Reading, Mass.: Addison-Wesley.

Truman, David B. (1951). *The Governmental Process*. New York: Knopf.

Useem, Michael (1979). "The social organization of the American business elite and participation of corporate directors in the governance of American institutions." *American Sociological Review* 44:553–572.

Useem, Michael (1984). *The Inner Circle: Large Corporations and the Rise of Business Political Activity in the U.S. and U.K.* New York: Oxford University Press.

Walker, Jack L. (1983). "The origins and maintenance of interest groups in America." *American Political Science Review* 77:390–406.

White, Harrison C., Boorman, Scott A., and Breiger, Ronald L. (1976). "Social structure from multiple networks, I: Block models of roles and positions." *American Journal of Sociology* 81:730–780.

Williamson, Oliver E. (1975). *Markets and Hierarchies: Analysis and Antitrust Implications*. New York: Free Press.

Williamson, Oliver E. (1981). "The economics of organizations: The transaction cost approach." *American Journal of Sociology* 87:548–577.

Williamson, Oliver E. (1985). *The Economic Institutions of Capitalism: Firms, Markets, Relational Contracting*. New York: Free Press.

Williamson, Peter J. (1985). *Varieties of Corporatism: A Conceptual Discussion*. London: Cambridge University Press.

Wilson, Graham (1982). "Why is there no corporatism in the United States?" In Gerhard Lehmbruch and Phillipps C. Schmitter (eds.), *Patterns of Corporatist Policymaking*. Beverly Hills, Calif. Sage Publications, pp. 219–236.

Wright, Erik Olin (1978). *Class, Crisis and the State*. London: New Left Books.

3 Organizational versus Class Components of Director Networks

Eugene Johnsen
Beth Mintz

The study of social power has long been a cornerstone of sociological investigation, and, at least since the work of Max Weber (1921), the organization has been viewed as the major seat of power in modern society. Attention to the role of the corporation in particular gained popularity in the United States in the 1930s when Berle and Means (1932) outlined the changing importance of organizational rule in their famous separation of ownership and control thesis.

Arguing that over the years the stock of the typical giant corporation has been widely dispersed, thus diluting the ownership interests of the founding families, they suggest that control of the modern corporation has passed from original owners to nonpropertied managers. And with this transformation, the power base of the traditional capitalist was thought to be severely undermined.

Contemporary research on stock ownership trends has confirmed some of Berle and Means' (1932) predictions. As they suggested, a vast majority of the very largest businesses in the United States are no longer family controlled firms (Zeitlin, 1974; Larner, 1970; Burch, 1972). Less clearcut, however, are the implications of this change for the traditional capitalist. While some have argued that the separation of ownership and control has solidified institutional power—power of position rather than the power of ownership—as the defining characteristic of modern society (Mills, 1956; Perrucci and Pilisuk, 1970; Dye, 1976), a parallel literature has emphasized the endurance of a capitalist class, united by common economic and social interests and solidified, at least theoretically, by conflict with subject classes (Domhoff, 1970, 1983; Zeitlin, 1980; Useem, 1984; Koenig and Gogel, 1981; Mintz, Freitag, Hendricks, and Schwartz, 1976).

While these perspectives assume extremely different dynamics of business organization, both concentrate on the corporation as the major unit of analysis and both have been using patterns of interlocking directorates to study the question of the location of power in the modern world. And this is the context within which the study of national corporate structures has gained popularity.

In the first instance, with an emphasis on institutional power, the corporation is viewed as an autonomous actor, unencumbered by ownership interests and thus able to independently strive to maintain its market position in the broadest possible sense. Resource dependency theory is a popular example of this type of approach. Assuming that corporate behavior is constrained, not by stockholders, but by the flow of resources necessary for the successful functioning of the firm,

57

this model argues that the modern corporation works to control these uncertainties in its environment (Aldrich and Pfeffer, 1976; Pfeffer and Salancik, 1978; Aldrich, 1979). Empirical investigations have analyzed the structure of relations among corporations in an attempt to understand the extremely complicated system of intercorporate interdependencies generated by these attempts at resource control (Perrucci and Pilisuk, 1970; Allen, 1974; Burt, 1979, 1980, 1983).

The study of the capitalist class, on the other hand, while emphasizing the importance of the corporation in the contemporary world, typically rejects the primacy of an institutional base of social power. Instead, work in this tradition often uses an organizational analysis to study questions of class structure and intraclass unity, an approach consistent with the assumption of property-based power. And although there are different approaches to the larger question of capitalist class formation, a common thread uniting this research is the assumption of elite involvement in corporate decision making.

There is disagreement about the exact relationship between class and organization in this context. While most agree that institutional position plays an important role in the identification of important actors, some researchers have viewed the corporation as part of a "class controlled apparatus of private appropriation" (Zeitlin, 1980:10), and this, of course, imputes primary importance to ownership as the ultimate source of power wielding. The class coordination model is consistent with this approach, assuming that class networks control both financial and nonfinancial firms (Ratcliff, 1980b). Even within this group, however, it is generally accepted that class structure is not solely based on family or personal relationships but "is buttressed by a massive network of institutional relationships" (Sweezy, quoted in Ratcliff, 1980b).

Others see a more equal merger of institutional and class relationships; an overlapping system with primacy left unspecified. Details vary by author: Domhoff (1970, 1979, 1983) emphasizes the cohesion generated by shared value systems and maintained by an interrelated set of social and institutional relationships. Useem (1984), too, stresses the social organization of the corporate community, underscoring the combination of institutional, ownership, and social components. He describes

> a set of interrelated, quasi-autonomous networks encompassing virtually all large corporations. Acquaintanceship circles, interlocking directorates, webs of interfirm ownership and major business associations are among the central strands of these networks. . . . But corporate credentials and upper-class origins are here subordinated to a distinct logic of classwide organization. (1984:14–15)

And classwide organization is the coincidence of class and corporate interests.

The idea of a merger of institutional and ownership power is quite appealing. Research has consistently demonstrated the upper class credentials of major corporate leaders. And although there are crucial differences between an upper and a capitalist class, this literature offers strong support for the interdependency notion.

At the same time, we do not have sufficient information to conclude that class and organization carry equal weight, or whether one set of relationships structures the second. The question that remains incompletely addressed, then, is: Given the importance of the organizational form in modern society and given the endurance of a visible capitalist class, how, precisely, do these two elements fit together? While evidence of interdependency is impressive, the details, thus far, remain unspecified.

Recent research has begun to investigate these issues. Mizruchi (1984) proposes an intercorporate theory of class cohesion that folds resource dependency theory into a social class model of organizational behavior. Galaskiewicz, Wasserman, Rauschenbach, Bielefeld, and Mullaney (1985:422), concentrating on the composition of the boards of directors of a group of companies in one geographic location, found that it is both the social credentials of executives *and* the market position of corporations that effect director recruitment patterns. Palmer, Friedland, and Singh (1986), on the other hand, found that on the local level class-based contacts may substitute for more formal corporate appointments as coordinating mechanisms among organizations.

Other work has approached the problem from different vantage points. Carroll (1985), in an investigation of the Canadian corporate system, analyzed the network of relations among directors rather than the more standard network of relations among corporations to examine this issue [1].

Bearden and Mintz (1987) used a similar approach in a study of the United States system. They found that both the corporate and director networks were important to the question of the relationship between class and organization in modern capitalism. They suggest, however, "that it is within the network of relations among directors where we see the overlap between institutional and class interests most clearly and where we must look for an understanding of the relationship between these two defining segments of American business structure" (p. 27).

Explicit in this conclusion is the identification of the director network as the primary location for investigating these issues. In addition, implicit in these remarks is the emphasis on a structural analysis as the appropriate framework within which to consider these questions. While investigations of director attributes have provided detailed and interesting portraits of high-level decision makers, analyses of intercorporate affairs have benefitted widely from studying patterned relationships among corporations. Bearden and Mintz suggest that the director network may well profit from similar techniques.

The present study follows these leads. It uses the network of interlocks among directors of the largest corporations in the United States to investigate the details of the relationship between class and organization in modern American society. It also takes seriously the importance of structure in social network analysis, in general, and in the specific case of the director network. Defining structure as "a recurrent pattern of social relations among social positions" (Laumann, Marsden, and Galaskiewicz, 1977:596), we assume that the network of relations among directors is more than the aggregation of a series of relations between pairs of directors and that the overall system constrains and orchestrates (Berkowitz, 1982) these relations. Thus, in the present study we use techniques of structural analysis to explore the exact relationship between class and organization in modern society.

The Logic of the Analysis

Investigations of interlocking directorates have a long history, although their application to the question of national corporate structures has increased dramatically in recent years [2]. Over time, these studies have been dominated by an organizational emphasis, concentrating on the firm as the unit of analysis. In these systems, however, there are actually two different networks to consider, each of which explores a different aspect of organizational and class relationships. Unlike the interlock network, the director or person network uses the individual as the typical unit of interest. Referred to as the dual of the corporate network (Breiger, 1974; see also Berkowitz, 1980, 1982), the director network investigates a different aspect of intercorporate relations and does so without assuming the primacy of the organizational form.

The Definition of the Director Network

The network of relations among directors is constructed from the more traditional system of interlocking directorates. Beginning with the definition of a link as a tie created when one individual sits on the board of directors of two or more companies, the director-by-director network is generated by reversing this relationship. While in the corporation network directors tie organizations into an interrelated system, the director network inverts this arrangement by viewing corporations as links that unite directors. Preliminary analysis suggests that the director network exhibits different structural properties from its dual, and that different parts of the system may be explored by its use (Breiger, 1974).

Since the person network is generated directly from the corporate network, this is the most ideal system with which to explore the relationship between organization and class in the business sector. Rather than defining the population of individuals under investigation by virtue of their social status or elite credentials, this procedure uses the corporation to define the study population.

Note, however, that the director network is not necessarily a good reflection of the intercorporate component of interlocking directorates. When individuals are defined as points, and corporations are defined as relationships connecting these points, not all directors—not even all interlockers—create direct intercorporate ties. In our data set (described later), for example, one director, George C. Kern, Jr., sat on the boards of Allied Stores and Babcock and Wilcox. A second director, George A. Roeder, Jr., also sat on the board of Allied Stores; he held a seat on Chase Manhattan, as well. Although Kern and Roeder were both interlockers and they were connected by their relationship with Allied Stores, this did not create a direct intercorporate tie. Individuals who sit on two boards together, on the other hand, create direct intercorporate ties and function as a director network equivalent of an interlocking directorate.

The definition of the person network, therefore, has various possibilities. In the present analysis, the director network includes all individuals in the system who sit together on at least two boards. Hence, it considers only those directors whose relationships establish intercorporate links. By defining the network in this way, we set the groundwork for generating a network of director interrelations with which to compare the more traditional network of intercorporate relationships. We note that this definition gives us a different vantage point from the system of all directors or all interlockers and hence different information is to be gained from the analysis.

The Definition of the Problem

Earlier analysis of the network of relations among directors has identified a system with a strong regional base overlaid by a national and a seminational grouping (Bearden and Mintz, 1987). Generated by a component analysis—the identification of all maximally connected subgroups—these findings suggest a regional nature to class organization as well as a hierarchically arranged system of director relationships. The national and seminational components include directors of national prominence, whereas the regional groupings are typically dominated by local elites. In all, nine groupings of size six or more were identified (see Table 3.1 for a description of the groups). Individuals included in the national and seminational components were headquartered in a variety of regions, but their connections to other directors transcended any regional base [3].

The grouped structure of the director network provides some interesting possibilities for exploring differences within the system of director relations. It supplies a set of matrices with which to compare network subsets and with which to investigate the relationship between organizational and class position.

The present study, therefore, takes advantage of information on the structure of the director network by analyzing the components within the system as

Table 3.1. Components of the Director Network

Region	Number of members	Number of social club members	Number of policy group members	Number in either a policy group or a social club
1. National	38	22	19	28
2. Seminational	21	13	3	13
3. New York (1)	18	10	3	13
4. Detroit	10	5	2	5
5. New York (2)	10	4	2	5
6. Pittsburgh	8	7	4	7
7. Boston	8	1	1	2
8. West Coast	7	4	1	4
9. Minneapolis	6	2	0	2
Total	126	68	35	79

separate networks and comparing the results. To do this, we model the two most important variables at issue, organizational position and class position, and we ask to what extent do social ties (class) order corporate (organizational) ties. We do this for the nine components described in Table 3.1, and we report our findings in three groupings: the national, the seminational, and the regional.

Corporate ties are defined by shared boardships: Two directors create an intercorporate link if they sit together on two or more boards. Class ties are defined in a variety of ways, all of which depend on social credentials rather than ownership interests. Although theoretically there are important differences between the social elite and the capitalist class, the former has been used successfully as a proxy for the latter repeatedly, and there is much evidence to suggest that the social elite is dominated by owners of the generalized means of production.

Specifically, following a long and rich tradition, class is defined in terms of social club and/or policy group membership (Domhoff, 1970, 1975, 1983; Ratcliff 1979–1980; Soref, 1976; Useem, 1978, 1984, each translated into a relational concept in a number of ways. We ask how ties to (or from) the elite organize shared boardships; how ties to *and* from the elite organize shared boardships; how ties among the elite organize shared boardships; and how ties within the elite and within the nonelite, taken together, organize shared boardships [4]. We further distinguish between shared elite status as defined by membership in any elite organization and shared status as defined by membership in the same organization. Elite status itself is broken down: We investigate separately the impact of social club membership, policy group membership, and membership in either of the two [5]. For each of the components listed in Table 3.1, we construct 15 matrixes modeling class status. These include: ties to (or from) social club members, signified as $.s$; ties to and from social club members, signified as $.s^+$; ties between social club members, signified as $.s^-$; and ties between social club members and between nonmembers, taken together, signified as $.cls$.

In addition, we model ties to (or from) policy group members $(.p)$; to and from policy group members $(.p^+)$; ties between policy group members $(.p^-)$; and between policy members and between nonpolicy members taken together $(.clp)$. We also investigate ties to (or from) a club or policy group member $(.a)$; to and from a club or policy member $(.a^+)$; between policy or club members $(.a^-)$; and between club or policy members and between nonclub nonpolicy group members, taken together. Finally, we include membership in the same social club $(.fs)$, the same policy group $(.fp)$, and either the same club or the same policy group $(.fa)$. This notation is summarized in Table 3.2. We compare these 15 to a corresponding organizational network (shared boardships) for each component using a method described later.

The Data

Data were collected on the boards of directors of 252 of the largest corporations in the United States for 1976. The list of firms include the 202

Table 3.2. Summary of Class Tie Network Definitions

Notation	Network ties
$.a$	To or from the elite[a]
$.a+$	To and from the elite
$.a-$	Among the elite
$.fa$	To the same elite organization
$.cla$	Among the elite and ties among nonelite considered together
$.s$	To or from social club members
$.s^+$	To and from social club members
$.s-$	Among social club members
$.fs$	To the same social club
$.cls$	Among social club members and ties among nonmembers considered together
$.p$	To or from policy group members
$.p+$	To and from policy group members
$.p-$	Among policy group members
$.fp$	To the same policy group
$.clp$	Among policy group members and among nonmembers considered together

[a] Elite is defined as either a social club or a policy group member.

largest nonfinancial corporations of all types for the year (as defined by sales) as well as the 50 largest financial institutions (as defined by assets) for the period as listed by *Fortune* magazine and supplemented by the "Forbes Sales 500." The data were originally collected as part of a larger study that compared corporate interlock patterns cross-nationally. While the techniques of data collection on interlocking directorates are by now quite standard, details about the data for this project can be found in Stokman, Ziegler, and Scott (1984).

Names of directors of the 252 corporations under investigation were obtained from the 1977 volume of *Standard and Poor's Register of Corporations, Directors, and Executives.* Information on elite characteristics of directors was obtained from *Who's Who in America* and from *The Social Register.*

Data Analysis

Data analysis for this chapter falls into two categories: the generation of components in the director network and an evaluation of the relationship between class position and organizational position within a series of networks. Components were identified by the computer package, GRADAP, which was specifically designed to address social network data. Developed in the Netherlands at the Universities of Amsterdam, Groningen, and Nijmegen, GRADAP is available for a wide range of social network problems [6]. The definition of components follows what is by now standard terminology for network analysis: A component of an undirected graph is a maximally connected subgraph (Stokman and van Veen, 1981:6). In the analyses that follow, we consider subgraphs of size 6 or larger. For details on the generation of components in interlock networks, see Stokman *et al.* (1984).

The present analysis explores the relationship between class and organization in modern capitalism and does so by evaluating the extent to which social relations and intercorporate relations are associated in the network of director ties. We use two different techniques to investigate this question. We begin with the more general problem of measuring the correspondence between two n by n matrixes, and we note that a variety of statistical methods are available for this type of analysis ranging from simple Contingency Table techniques to some sophisticated weighted regression and log linear models. While these offer the possibility of measuring the correlation between class and organizational variables as we have defined them, they ignore any structural property implicit in the data.

Suppose, for example, that there is a systematic patterning in the way that shared elite status is distributed in a particular region. Assume, perhaps, that two directors are both members of the same social club and that they share membership on two corporate boards. In this case, there is a correspondence between shared club membership and shared board status. Assume, further, that one of the directors also belongs to the same club as a third director. Does this additional relationship impact on the original relation between the first two, or is it completely independent? Put another way, do the internal social linkages of a board member—the overall set of directors with whom he/she links—condition or contribute to that director's shared board memberships?

Traditional measures of conformity do not incorporate this type of information on the structural properties of the data. Instead, most techniques compare the number of corresponding entries in Matrix A and Matrix B, for example, how many times a 1 in cell ij of Matrix A is accompanied by a 1 in cell ij of Matrix B, with a randomized matching of cell entries. This procedure assumes the independence of each entry and that all $[n(n-1)]!$ orderings of a matrix are of equal likelihood when compared to the fixed ordering of the matrix with which it is compared.

Our emphasis on structure and our interest in incorporating structural properties into our analysis sensitizes us to the limitations of this type of approach. Thus, in the present investigation, we use a technique that tests for the presence of a similarity of patterning between two networks, while incorporating information on the internal tie structure of each director. Termed Quadratic Assignment (QA), this method measures the statistical association between two matrixes without sacrificing data on the specific patterning of an individual's links. In our case, we use it to control for the abstract tie structure of our networks of class relationships while comparing each to its organizational counterpart. Rather than a random matching of cell entries, QA compares two matrixes by permuting the row and column labels of one matrix and measuring the cell correspondence with a second, fixed, matrix. The null hypothesis assumes that all $n!$ possible relabelings are equally likely.

Figure 3.1 illustrates this procedure. A is the matrix representation of the shared board membership of three corporate directors. B_1 represents the shared club memberships ($.fs$) of the same three individuals and, following Hubert and Baker (1978), N_{AB_1} is the number of entries in A and B_1 that are both defined by 1s. While holding A constant, we randomize the entries in B_1 by permuting the

A				B_1				B_2				B_3				B_4				B_5				B_6		
	1	*2*	*3*		*1*	*2*	*3*		*3*	*2*	*1*		*1*	*3*	*2*		*2*	*3*	*1*		*2*	*1*	*3*		*3*	*1*	*2*
1	0	1	1	1	0	1	0	3	0	1	0	1	0	0	1	2	0	1	1	2	0	1	1	3	0	0	1
2	1	0	0	2	1	0	1	2	1	0	1	3	0	0	1	3	1	0	0	1	1	0	0	1	0	0	1
3	1	0	0	3	0	1	0	1	0	1	0	2	1	1	0	1	1	0	0	3	1	0	0	2	1	1	0

	$N_{AB_1}=2$	$N_{AB_2}=2$	$N_{AB_3}=2$	$N_{AB_4}=4$	$N_{AB_5}=4$	$N_{AB_6}=2$

Figure 3.1. Comparison between shared board membership (A) and all possible row and column relabelings of the matrix of shared social club status (B_1).

rows and columns of B_1, and we then compare each permutation to the fixed A. We do this *n!* times and compare the original inner product—N_{AB_1}—to all possible results as calculated from *N!* reorderings. Thus in the example shown in Figure 3.1, six possible row and column labelings exist, and this defines the population of inner product sums with which to compare the original relationship [7].

Significance levels are calculated by comparing the inner product value of the original configuration with all possible inner products [8]. We use a one-tailed test to evaluate the probability of independence between each set of two matrixes. In addition, when the original inner product corresponds to either the maximum or minimum values of the distribution of all possible inner products, the patterning of the relationship between the two networks mathematically cannot be any stronger. We use this information to supplement our traditional reliance on significance testing as the major indicator of the existence of a relationship [9]. We use the notation *ipo, ipmax,* and *ipmin* to refer to the original inner product, the maximum value of any inner product included in the distribution, and the minimum value in the distribution, respectively.

Finally, a strong form of tie patterning between two networks occurs when every interpersonal tie in one network is reflected as a corresponding tie in the other network. When this happens, the first network is said to be contained in the second. This relationship is illustrated in Figure 3.2. Note that for every entry 1 in A, there is a corresponding entry 1 in B, although not every entry 1 of B is reflected in A. Since A is contained in B, we know that B impacts on A rather than vice versa. Thus, this pattern suggests that B structures A.

We use this information to impute causality to our analyses. While quadratic assignment identifies those relationships that are associated, the containment patterns identify the direction of the relationship. Although this type of strong tie patterning is not always accompanied by a significant association in QA, it *always* produces an *ipo = ipmax*, which is the strongest positive mathematical relationship possible between two networks.

Thus, we use this information to supplement QA by addressing the direction of the relationship between class and organizational variables. We indicate these relationships by specifying the two relevant networks (in abbreviated form) separated by the following symbol: ⊂. We use *org* to represent the matrix of

A	B
0 1 1 1 1	0 1 1 1 1
1 0 0 0 1	1 0 0 0 1
1 1 0 0 0	1 1 0 1 1
0 0 0 0 0	0 0 0 0 0
1 1 0 0 0	1 1 0 0 0

Figure 3.2. Containment relation: Every entry 1 in A is reflected in B.

shared board membership and we append it to a shortened version of the component name. Thus, $nat.org \subset nat.s^+$ indicates that in the national component, every organizational tie between two directors is reflected by a tie to and from a social club member. We would conclude from this that in the national system under investigation, class relations—as measured by ties to social club members—structure organizational relations.

In addition, if all but one tie of one network is reflected in the other, then we indicate this by the *almost* containment relation, and if all but a maximum of 5% of one set of ties is contained in the other, we indicate this as an *approximate* containment relation. The containment, almost containment, and approximate containment relations are noted when they occur.

We summarize our results for the various components in Table 3.3. We present significance levels for all analyses in which $p \leq .10$. In addition, we use an X to indicate that the null hypothesis of independence has not been rejected using the one-tail test mentioned previously, but the relationship is of interest nevertheless, because $ipo = ipmin$ or $ipmax$. Information on whether the association is positive or negative is also included, as is indications of any containment relationships.

Results

The National Component

The national component is composed of corporate directors who, as a group, are more cosmopolitan than their regional and seminational counterparts. They tend to be bank directors, members of both elite social clubs and policy planning groups, and insiders in the largest corporations in the United States. As Table 3.1 illustrates, of the 38 individuals in the network, 28 are members of the general elite (a), 22 belong to elite social clubs (s), and 19 are affiliated with important policy planning organizations (p).

When we convert these attributes to relational data and ask which set of social tie relationships are associated with intercorporate links, we find that two definitions of intraclass relationships are positively associated with shared board status ($p < .05$): membership in the *same* social club ($.fs$) and membership in either the *same* social club or the *same* policy group ($.fa$).

Looking at the distribution of possible inner product sums does not add information to this analysis. However, when we relax the criterion for significance a bit, we find a positive association between intraclass social club ties ($.cls$) and intercorporate links ($p<.09$) indicating that similarity of status vis-à-vis club membership is related to shared board membership. Specifically, when two directors sit on the same boards, they tend both to be either club members or nonclub members, rather than a mixture of the two.

Table 3.3. Statistical Characteristics of the Components

Social ties	QA ipo^b	Direct. of Assoc.	QA $p < .10$	Containment relationships
National				
.fa	34	+	.04	*nat.org $\subset$ nat.a$^+$*
.fs	22	+	.05	*approx*
.cls	56	+	.09	
Seminational				
.fa	28*	+	.001	*semi.org $\subset$ semi.np$^+$*
.s	42	+	.06	*almost*
.s$^-$	34	+	.01	
.fs	26*	+	.001	
.cls	42	+	.01	

Social ties		QA ipo^b	Direct. of Assoc.	QA $p < .10$	Containment relationships
Regions					
.s$^+$	New York (2)^c	18*	+	.04	*NY(1).org $\subset$ NY(1).np$^+$*
	Minneapolis	12*	+	.03	
	West	14*	+	X	*Det.org $\subset$ Det.np$^+$*
	Boston	14*	+	X	
.s	Minneapolis	7*	+	.03	*NY(2).org $\subset$ NY(2).np$^+$*
	New York (2)	11	+	.07	*Pitt.org $\subset$ Pitt.np$^+$*
	Pittsburgh	19	+	X	*almost*
	Boston	7*	+	X	
.s$^-$	Pittsburgh	18*	+	X	*West.org $\subset$ West.s$^+$*
	Minneapolis	2*	+	X	*Minn.org $\subset$ Minn.s$^+$*
.cls	New York (1)^c	20*	−	.05	*NY(2).org $\subset$ NY(2).s$^+$*
	Pittsburgh	18*	+	X	*almost*
	Minneapolis	2	−	.07	*Pitt.org $\subset$ Pitt.fs*
	Boston	20	−	X	*almost*
.fs	New York (1)	12	+	.10	*NY(2).org $\subset$ NY(2).a$^+$*
	Pittsburgh	18*	+	X	*almost*
	Minneapolis	2*	+	X	*Bost.s$^+$ $\subset$ Bost.org*
					Bost.s $\subset$ Bost.org
					Bost.a$^-$ $\subset$ Bost.org
					Minn.s$^-$ $\subset$ Minn.org

[a] For social tie network definitions, see Table 3.2.

[b] *ipo* refers to the original inner product of the interlock and social tie networks. If *ipo* is equal to either the maximum or minimum values of the inner product statistic in its distribution, it is indicated by an asterisk.

[c] See designations in Table 3.1.

When we use a moderately strong definition of significance, then, we find that three sets of social relationships are associated with shared board memberships in the national component: .fs, .fa, and .cls. These findings are summarized in Table 3.3, which also includes information on significance levels, inner product distributions (*ipo* = *ipmax* or *ipmin*) where relevant, as well as a list of the containment relationships present.

We are surprised by the relationships identified in this analysis, most particularly by the association between membership in the same organization and shared boardships. Given the national stature of the directors under investigation in this grouping, we expected general club membership or general elite status rather than specific shared memberships to be of import. This assumes that national prominence transcends possible face to face relationships, and that general class position is related to the formation of intercorporate links.

Although this assumption is not supported by the networks defined as .fs and .fa, the relationship between intraclass ties (.cls) and shared boardships is of interest in this context. The positive association between shared social club membership and shared nonmembership, on the one hand, and shared board-ships, on the other, suggests that intraclass links on the general level are also of interest in this grouping.

From this analysis, we conclude that social ties *are* associated with shared board membership, and that on the national level, both membership in the same club and club membership status in general is important. And we note that social club relationships are of more interest in this process than policy groupings since those networks that were defined only in terms of policy affiliations were not associated with shared interorganizational links.

Finally, there is one approximate containment relationship identified in the national system: Nearly every interlock tie (95.7%) is reflected as a tie to and from an elite ($nat.org_{approx} \subseteq nat.a^{+}$). This indicates that social relationships—ties to and from either club members or policy group members, specifically—pattern intercorporate ties. Thus we interpret this relationship as causal and we argue that, in this system, one's relationship to members of the social elite contributes to the formation of intercorporate links. This suggests that for the national component, class offers an important contribution to interorganizational relations while interorganizational patterns do not impact on class relations.

The Seminational Component

Earlier analysis of the component structure of the network of relations among directors found that the seminational grouping did not fit squarely into either the regional or the national arena (Bearden and Mintz, 1987). Although a majority of the members were based in Chicago (*n* = 14), others came from the Minneapolis–St. Paul area ($n = 4$), the far west ($n = 2$) or New York ($n = 1$). And while its strong midwestern orientation suggested less than national stature, its diversity differentiated it from the more strictly regional groupings to be discussed later.

Other characteristics of directors in the component support this in-between status. These individuals tend to be bank directors, and many belong to elite social clubs. Few, however, are policy group members. Of the 21 directors in the component, 13 are members of the general elite (a), the same 13 belong to elite social clubs (s) and three sit on important policy planning boards (p) (Table 3.1). Because *.a* and *.s* are the same, different values for these categories are possible for only *.fa* and *.fs*; we report results for *.s* rather than *.a*.

As Table 3.3 indicates, the seminational component shares some similarities with the national system. Here we find significant positive associations between interlock ties and: ties among members of the same club (*.fs*), ties among members of the same club or the same policy group (*.fa*), and intraclass social club ties (*.cls*); and for the first two, this is also supported by *ipo = ipmax*. In addition, interlock ties are positively associated with links among the social club elite (*.s⁻*). And when we relax our criterion for significance slightly, ties to (or from) social club members (*.s*) are also positively associated with shared board membership ($p = .06$).

Thus, within the seminational component, social club ties are again found to be important vis-à-vis shared boardships and, hence, to the creation of intercorporate links. And the relevance of both general (*.cls*) and specific (*.fs, .fa*) shared social relations identified in the national system is present in this network as well. Moreover, as in the larger system, our analysis did not identify any significant associations involving policy group members, suggesting that social club and policy group memberships function differently in relation to the formation of interorganizational ties.

In fact, the only relationship identified within the seminational component that speaks to the role of policy groups is a negative one: We found that *semi.org* $\underset{\text{almost}}{\subseteq}$ *semi.np⁺* indicating that all but one of the intercorporate ties found within the component *must* be formed by a pair that includes at least one director who is not a policy board member. We can interpret this result in two ways, but first we note that this relationship indicates directionality: Policy group membership—or lack of it in this case—impacts on shared board positions rather than shared board status patterning policy group membership. Hence, in this case, it is the policy planning element that organizes intercorporate relations and not visa versa.

Given this information, at first glance it seems as if membership in a prestigious policy planning group discourages board recruitment, at least for those directors who form intercorporate links. However, since almost every pair of directors who share board membership includes an individual who is not a member of a policy group, this suggests instead that board recruitment occurs largely within the nonpolicy elite and that membership in important policy groups is unnecessary in the seminational arena. Thus, while social club contacts—both direct and indirect—are associated with the creation of intercorporate ties, policy group affiliations seem to function in a different way. From this we speculate that the relationship between social club membership and the formation of intercorporate links is based on the general integrating role that shared social status provides. Policy group membership, on the other hand, seems to perform a more specific function, one that is probably rooted in the conflict resolution that these groups are thought to supply.

Our results, therefore, are consistent with previous research that has suggested that recruitment occurs between social clubs and corporate boards, especially among those directors who create interorganizational ties. They also distinguish between shared club and policy group memberships, underscoring the differences in the way these relations are organized vis-à-vis the creation of corporate interlocks.

At the same time, our results point to differences in the organization of social contacts. When we compare the national and seminational levels, we find that for the latter, in addition to the importance of face-to-face associations suggested by membership in the same club, membership in any of a selection of elite clubs is relevant to board recruitment. Thus, our findings suggest that it is on the national level where membership in the same club is most important. When we leave the national scene, alternative networks appear to become relevant in relation to director contacts.

The Regional Components

Although there is variation among regional networks in terms of the proportion of directors who are members of elite organizations (see Table 3.1), as well as the specific definitions of class relationships that are associated with interorganizational links, some general patterns emerge when we consider the regional system as a whole, and these patterns distinguish regional networks from their national and seminational counterparts.

While in the national and seminational components, membership in the same organization is associated with shared boardships, face to face contact of that sort does not characterize the regional system in the same way. Instead within the regions, ties to members of any elite social club are most often associated with shared board membership, and, thus, ties to those of social elite status on the general level are typically related to the creation of intercorporate links.

Specifically, we find significant positive associations between shared board memberships and ties to (or from) social club members ($.s$), as well as ties to and from social club members ($.s^+$). In addition, in two of the regions, ties among social club members ($.s^-$) are arranged such that *ipo = ipmax,* indicating that the patterning of the relationship between shared social club membership and shared board membership mathematically cannot be stronger.

These findings indicate that the formation of intercorporate links is related to the patterning of ties of those directors affiliated with the most exclusive and prestigious social clubs in the world. They also indicate, however, that the specific types of relationships to social club members that are associated with the creation of interorganizational ties is not constant across all regions. In the regional networks, one's status relation to a social club member is more important than shared membership in the same social club, and this distinguishes the regional system from the broader based national network.

Other differences between groupings exist, as well. In the seminational system, there is a positive association between the creation of intercorporate links and ties among social club members and ties among nonmembers when considered together ($.cls$) which is also identified in the national component if we relax our criterion for significance ($p = .09$) a bit. Within the regions, we find that in three out of four components (larger New York, Boston, and Minneapolis) there is a significant ($p \leq .07$ in two of them) association between these matrixes, but the relationships are negative, suggesting that in terms of intraclass connections as defined by shared social club status and the formation of intercorporate ties, one set of relationships discourages the other.

Moreover, these findings reinforce our original analysis which argued that the system of intercorporate ties generated by directors who share board membership can be divided into two distinct groups, with a third occupying a mid-range position. In the seminational component, membership in the same social club ($.fs$), shared social club status ($.s^-$), as well as ties to social club members ($.s$) are associated with the formation of interorganizational connections. In the national system, a director's own position as a social club member is as important as his or (very rarely) her relation to social club members, since shared club membership ($.fs$) is associated with the formation of intercorporate ties. And in the regional system, of course, the status relations to social club members are the most relevant ones identified. However, in all systems it is relationships to social club members and not policy board affiliates that are associated with the creation of interorganizational relationships.

Finally, within the regional groupings, containment relationships offer some striking evidence with which to evaluate causality in reference to class versus organizational variables. As Table 3.3 indicates, elite class relations pattern interorganizational relations in three of the seven regional systems under investigation in the present analysis. In an additional grouping, both class and organization were found to be causal in reference to different variables, and in only one locale, Boston, did intercorporate ties alone pattern elite class relations. We begin with a consideration of our most anomalous result.

Directors included in the Boston region are drawn primarily from three locally headquartered major companies (John Hancock, Raytheon, and First Boston Corporation), and as a group, these individuals tend not to be elite. Of the eight members, only two are defined as socially elite, one of whom belongs to a social club while the other is affiliated with a prestigious policy planning group. While QA did not identify any associations between class and organizational variables that were statistically significant in this component, the inner product distributions generated from measuring the correspondence between ties to and/or from social club members ($.s$, $.s^+$) and shared board memberships were found to be at a mathematical maximum. This relationship is reflected in the results of the containment analysis. In both cases, as well as for $.a^-$, social tie relations are found to be patterned by intercorporate ties, suggesting that in this system, interorganizational relations contribute to social relations.

In only one other instance, Minneapolis, do we find organizational relationships patterning social relationships, and in this case, interpretation is much less clearcut. This is the smallest grouping under investigation, and only two of the six members of the component are defined as elite. An additional two, Bruce and Kenneth Dayton of Dayton–Hudson, seem to be excellent candidates for inclusion in an ownership class. While this points to the limitations of operationalizing class in terms of social attributes, analysis of the relations among these directors produces some interesting results.

Since the elite directors both belong to the same social clubs and no one in the grouping belongs to a policy planning committee, then $.s^- = .fs$, $.s = .a$, and $.p = 0$. Results indicate that there are significant positive associations between ties to and/or from club members ($.s^+$, $.s$) and shared board ties. Additionally, for $.s^-$, $ipo = ipmax$ pointing to a relationship between shared club membership status and the creation of intercorporate links. Taken together, these findings suggest that for the Minneapolis–St. Paul component, ties that involve social club members are associated with interlock ties, and that shared club membership status is probably important as well. When we use containment relations to impute causality, however, our results are contradictory. We find that $minn.org \subset minn.s^+$ and $minn.s^- \subset minn.org$ indicating that while ties to and from club members organize intercorporate links, intercorporate links organize shared club membership status. When we note that the matrix $.s^-$ contains only two entries, we are tempted to emphasize the finding that social relationships pattern organizational relationships, but we emphasize caution in such an interpretation.

More important, in the Minneapolis area, the exact relationship between class and organizational variables is unclear, leaving just one locale (Boston) in which intercorporate ties were incontrovertably found to organize social relationships. In three other of the seven components, on the other hand, social relationships, variables that were used to model class relations, were found to organize the formation of intercorporate links, suggesting that class relations still, in the latter part of the twentieth century, exert important influence on the formation of interorganizational linkages while interorganizational linkages do not exert comparable influence on class relations. We consider this a major finding, and we now turn to an exploration of the circumstances under which class relations organize intercorporate relations.

Within the regional systems, the set of relations that were found to impact on the formation of interorganizational ties most frequently were ties to and from directors who were not members of prestigious policy planning groups ($.np^+$). This is true in both New Yorks and Detroit, trivially true in Boston, the West, and Minneapolis, while in Pittsburgh, all but one of the interorganizational links is contained in $.np^+$. Thus, in all seven regions—as well as in the seminational system —intercorporate ties are formed by pairs of directors that include at least one nonpolicy board member. These results indicate that a director's relationship to directors excluded from important policy planning boards organize shared corporate board memberships and, thus, organize the establishment of intercorporate links. Our most consistent finding, then, is that a director's relationship to policy board members impacts on the formation of intercorporate ties, and we interpret this to suggest that participants in the broad, economic, policy planning process are placed on corporate boards very carefully so that representation is not duplicated. Moreover, we speculate from this that policy board members may be the true diplomats of the intercorporate network.

The second most frequent set of social relations found to organize the development of intercorporate links are ties to and from social club members. This characterizes the smaller New York and West components as well as the less understood Minneapolis system. In addition, ties to and from either a social club member or a policy group member organize the formation of intercorporate links in one area (smaller New York), and in an additional component, Pittsburgh, ties among same club members are causal in this regard. These findings again distinguish the regional systems from the national and seminational components where one's relationship to social club members rarely organizes intercorporate links. Moreover, these results underscore the importance of social club contacts to the formation of interorganizational connections and indicate that ties to and from members of the social elite are most important in the creation of interorganizational relations.

Conclusion

Our investigation of the relationship between class and organization within the corporate world was designed to address an increasingly important question in interorganizational analysis: Given the prominence of the organizational form in modern industrial society and given the endurance of a visible capitalist class, how precisely do these elements fit together? Although we have only scratched the surface of such an analysis, we have identified a fairly consistent set of social relationships that are associated with the formation of interorganizational links.

By way of summary, we reiterate the following points: (1) social relationships, elite club memberships in particular, are associated with shared board memberships and, hence, with the formation of intercorporate links; (2) social club memberships function differently from policy group affiliations in relation to the formation of intercorporate links; (3) regional networks are organized differently from the more cosmopolitan national system while the seminational grouping shares characteristics with each; (4) while interorganizational ties were found to pattern class relationships in some of our analyses, more frequently variables used to model class relationships were found to pattern interorganizational ties.

From our findings, we conclude, first, that social class does, indeed, function as a recruiting mechanism for corporate directors, especially for those directors who create interorganizational links. The recruitment process is not identical in all parts of the network, however. On the national level, those contacts most closely associated with the formation of intercorporate relations are face to face, suggesting that here, elite clubs or policy planning groups serve to identify and bring together a viable population for recruitment purposes. On the regional level, on the other hand, these sorts of shared social memberships do not seem to play the same role. We speculate from these differences that on the regional level, well defined but less formal social networks function in identifying likely board candidates.

Second, in our analysis of the seminational system, we suggested that the differences between ties formed by social club members and ties of policy group members, as they relate to the formation of intercorporate links, may be interpreted to indicate that social club members play a general integrating role while policy group affiliates serve a more specific function. After combining information generated in the national, seminational, and regional groupings, we conclude that there is indeed a division of labor between these organizations. While the relation between ties to social club members and the formation of interorganizational links seems to revolve around supplying an available pool of potential recruits, it is clear that policy planning membership does not function in this way. Instead, our findings may indicate that directors who are members of important policy planning organizations are more carefully placed in the corporate community, and the peculiar relationship between ties involving these individuals and the formation of intercorporate links reflects this arrangement.

Finally, and most critically, we emphasize that social formations are more important in the creation of interorganizational ties than interorganizational ties are for the creation of social relations. This suggests that while the merger of institutional and class relationships identified in recent studies of the structure of the capitalist class is, indeed, accurate, the merger is not an equal one. Instead, class formations are found to take precedence. To the extent that the social relations used in the present study serve as adequate proxies for class relations, our findings underscore the continued importance of property-based power in the age of postindustrial society.

Moreover, since class processes impact in this way on economic processes, the image of the organizational form as separated from a class-based system of social relations is not supported by our results. Instead, our findings point to the possibility that ownership remains the ultimate source of power wielding, and that the institutional base of social power suggested by many organizational theories may be overstated.

Notes

1. See Bonacich and Domhoff (1981) for a network analysis that maps groups and people and analyzes the relation between the two.

2. For examples of recent interlock studies, see Allen (1974); Bearden, Atwood, Freitag, Hendricks, Mintz, and Schwartz (1975); Bunting (1976); Burt (1979, 1980); Fennema (1982); Levine (1972); Mariolis (1975); Mintz and Schwartz (1981, 1985); Mizruchi (1982, 1983); Ornstein (1982); Palmer (1983); Roy (1983); Sonquist and Koenig (1975). For reviews of interlock research see Soref (1979) and Fennema and Schijf (1979); for a social history see DiDonnata, Glasberg, Mintz, and Schwartz (1988).

3. See Bearden and Mintz (1987) for a full description of the data, the methods, and the findings.

4. Matrixes modeling ties to (or from) the elite contain 1s as column entries for each elite director; ties to and from the elite contain 1s as row and column entries for each elite director; ties among the elite contain 1s in the ijth cells for the elite pairs; and ties among the elite and among the nonelite, taken together, contain 1s in ijth cells for the elite pairs and for the nonelite pairs. In all cases, entries $ii = 0$.

5. A core list of elite social clubs and policy planning groups was taken from Domhoff (1970) and supplemented with listings from Bonacich and Domhoff (1977).

6. For information on availability contact: Prof. dr. F.N. Stokman, Sociologisch Instituut, Rijksuniversiteit, Oude Boteringestraat 23, 9712 GC Groningen, The Netherlands.

7. QA probabilities are calculated in three ways: by the generation of the permutation distributions of inner products using all possible matrix relabelings, which we call QAP; by a random sampling (with replacement) of the $n!$ permutations for larger networks which we indicate as QAS; and by formula, to which we refer as QAF.

QAP generates the exact distribution of inner product sums using all $n!$ permutations of the row and column assignments (done simultaneously) of the n members in a social tie system. Since the value of $n!$ rapidly becomes very large as the size of the network increases, we are able to use QAP only for groups of size 8 or less, which in the present study includes Boston, Pittsburgh, West Coast, and Minneapolis. When n is greater than 8, this distribution is approximated by a random sample of the $n!$ permutations. In these cases, we use a sample ranging from 2400 to 5040 permutations, and we refer to the procedure as QAS.

Finally, QAF calculates the mean and standard deviation of the distribution of inner product sums generated by comparing a fixed A (organizational relationships) with all possible relabelings of B (class relationships).

We have cross-checked QAS with QAP for networks of size 8 or less, and QAS with QAF for larger systems and found that the permutation distributions generated by QAS and QAP were quite close as were the means and standard deviations calculated by QAS and QAF.

8. See Burt (1982) for a discussion of significance testing in this context.

9. Cases in which the social network matrix (elite ties) contains either all 1s or all 0s in its off-diagonal cells generate only one value for the product and hence are trivial. These are excluded from consideration.

References

Aldrich, Howard (1979). *Organizations and Environments*. Englewood Cliffs: Prentice Hall.

Aldrich, Howard, and Pfeffer, Jeffrey (1976). "Environments of organizations." *Annual Review of Sociology* 2:79–105.

Allen, Michael (1974). "Interorganizational elite cooptation." *American Sociological Review* 39:393–406.

Bearden, James, Atwood, William, Freitag, Peter, Hendricks, Carol, Mintz, Beth, and Schwartz, Michael (1975). "The nature and extent of bank centrality in corporate networks." Paper presented at the Meetings of the American Sociological Association, Chicago.

Bearden, James, and Mintz, Beth (1987). "The structure of class cohesion: The corporate network and its dual." In M. Mizruchi and M. Schwartz (eds.), *Structural Analysis*. Cambridge: Cambridge University Press.

Berkowitz, S.D. (1980). "Structural and non-structural models of elites: A critique." *Canadian Journal of Sociology* 5(1):13–30.

Berkowitz, S.D. (1982). *An Introduction to Structural Analysis: The Network Approach to Social Research*. Toronto: Butterworths.

Berle, Adolph, and Means, Gardiner (1932). *The Modern Corporation and Private Property*. New York: Harcourt, Brace and World.

Bonacich, Phillip, and Domhoff, G. William (1977). "Overlapping memberships among eight clubs and policy groups of the American ruling class: A methodological and empirical contribution to the class hegemony paradigm of power structure." Paper presented at the meetings of the American Sociological Association, Chicago, 1977.

Bonacich, Phillip, and Domhoff, G. William (1981). "Latent classes and group membership." *Social Networks* 3:175–196.

Breiger, Ronald (1974). "The duality of persons and groups." *Social Forces* 53:181–190.

Bunting, David (1976). "Corporate interlocking." *The Journal of Corporate Action* 1:6–15.

Burch, Philip, Jr. (1972). *The Managerial Revolution Reassessed.* Lexington: D.C. Heath.

Burt, Ronald (1979). "A structural theory of interlocking corporate directorates." *Social Networks* 1:415–435.

Burt, Ronald (1980). "Cooptive corporate actor networks: A reconsideration of interlocking directorates involving American manufacturing." *Administrative Science Quarterly* 25:557–582.

Burt, Ronald (1982). *Toward a Structural Theory of Action.* New York: Academic Press.

Burt, Ronald (1983). *Corporate Profits and Cooptation.* New York: Academic Press.

Carroll, William K. (1985). "The individual, class, and corporate power in Canada." *Canadian Journal of Sociology* 9:245–268.

DiDonnata, Donna, Glasberg, Davita, Mintz, Beth, and Schwartz, Michael. (1988). "Theories of corporate interlocks: A social history." In Sam Bacharach and Nancy Di Tomaso, eds., *Research in the Sociology of Organizations,* Vol. 6. Greenwich, CT, JAI Press.

Domhoff, G. William (1970). *The Higher Circles.* New York: Random House.

Domhoff, G. William (1975). "Social clubs, policy-planning groups and corporations." *Insurgent Sociologist* 5:173–184.

Domhoff, G. William (1979). *The Powers That Be.* New York: Random House.

Domhoff, G. William (1983). *Who Rules America Now?* Englewood Cliffs, N.J.: Prentice Hall.

Dye, Thomas R. (1976). *Who's Running America?* Englewood Cliffs, N.J.: Prentice Hall.

Fennema, Meindert (1982). *International Networks of Banks and Industry.* Boston: Martinus Nijhoff.

Fennema, Meindert, and Schijf, B. (1979). "Analyzing interlocking directorates: Theory and methods." *Social Networks* 1:297–332.

Galaskiewicz, Joseph, Wasserman, Stanley, Rauschenbach, Barbara, Bielefeld, Wolfgang, and Mullaney, Patti (1985). "The influence of corporate power, social status, and market position on corporate interlocks in a regional network." *Social Forces* 64:403–431.

Glasberg, Davita (1981). "Corporate power and control: The case of Leasco Corporation versus Chemical Bank." *Social Problems* 29:104–116.

Herman, Edward (1981). *Corporate Control, Corporate Power.* New York: Cambridge University Press.

Hubert, Lawrence, and Baker, Frank (1978). "Evaluating the conformity of sociometric measurements." *Psychometrika* 43:31–41.

Keeping, E.S. (1962). *Introduction to Statistical Inference*. Princeton, N.J.: D. Van Nostrand Co., Inc.

Koenig, Tom, and Gogel, Robert (1981). "Interlocking directorates as a social network." *American Journal of Economics and Sociology* 40:37–50.

Kotz, David (1978). *Bank Control of Large Corporations in the United States*. Berkeley: University of California Press.

Larner, Robert (1970). *Management Control and the Large Corporation*. New York: Dunellen Pub. Co.

Laumann, Edward, Marsden, Peter, and Galaskiewicz, Joseph (1977). "Community-elite influence structures: Extension of a network approach." *American Journal of Sociology* 83:594–631.

Levine, Joel (1972). "The sphere of influence." *American Sociological Review* 37:14–27.

Mariolis, Peter (1975). "Interlocking directorates and the control of corporations." *Social Science Quarterly* 56:425–439.

Mills, C. Wright (1956). *The Power Elite*. New York: Oxford University Press.

Mintz, Beth, and Schwartz, Michael (1981). "The structure of intercorporate unity in American business." *Social Problems* 29:87–103.

Mintz, Beth, and Schwartz, Michael (1985). *The Power Structure of American Business*. Chicago: University of Chicago Press.

Mintz, Beth, Freitag, Peter, Hendricks, Carol, and Schwartz, Michael (1976). "Problems of proof in elite research." *Social Problems* 23:314–324.

Mizruchi, Mark (1982). *The American Corporate Network: 1904–1974*. Beverly Hills: Sage.

Mizruchi, Mark (1983). "The structure of relations among large American corporations." *Social Science History* 7:165–182.

Mizruchi, Mark (1984). "An interorganizational model of class cohesion." *Power and Elites* 1:23–36.

Ornstein, Michael (1982). "Interlocking directorate in Canada: Evidence from replacement patterns." *Social Networks* 4:3–25.

Palmer, Donald (1983). "On the significance of interlocking directorates." *Social Science History* 7:217–231.

Palmer, Donald, Friedland, Roger, and Singh, Jitendra V. (1986). "Stability in a corporate interlock network." *American Sociological Review* 51:781–796.

Perrucci, Robert, and Pilisuk, Marc (1970). "Leaders and ruling elites: The interorganizational bases of community power." *American Sociological Review* 35:1040–1057.

Pfeffer, Jeffrey, and Salanick, Gerald (1978). *The External Control of Organizations: A Resource Dependence Perspectives*. New York: Harper & Row.

Ratcliff, Richard (1979–1980). "Capitalist class structure and the decline of older industrial cities." *Insurgent Sociologist* 9:60–74.

Ratcliff, Richard (1980). "Banks and corporate lending: An analysis of the impact of the internal structure of the capitalist class." *American Sociological Review* 45:553–570. (a)

Ratcliff, Richard (1980). "Banks and the command of capital flows." In M. Zeitlin (ed.), *Classes, Class Conflict and the State*. Cambridge, Mass: Winthrop. (b)

Roy, William (1983). "The interlocking directorate structure of the United States." *American Sociological Review* 48:243–257.

Scott, John P. (1979). *Corporations, Classes, and Capitalism.* London: Hutchinson.

Sonquist, John, and Koenig, Thomas (1975). "Interlocking directorates in the top U.S. corporations: A graph theory approach." *Insurgent Sociologist* 5:196–230.

Soref, Michael (1976). "Social class and a division of labor within the corporate elite." *Sociological Quarterly* 17:360–368.

Soref, Michael (1979). "Research on interlocking directorates: An introduction and a bibliography of North American sources." *Connections* 2:84–86.

Stokman, F.N., and van Veen, F.J.A.M. (1981). *Gradap: Graph Definition and Analysis Package User's Manual,* Volume 2. Amsterdam: University of Amsterdam.

Stokman, F.N., Zeigler, Rolf, and Scott, John (1984). *Corporations and Corporate Power.* Oxford: Polity Press.

Useem, Michael (1978). "The inner group of the American capitalist class." *Social Problems* 25:225–240.

Useem, Michael (1984). *The Inner Circle: Large Corporations and the Rise of Business Political Activity in the U.S. and U.K.* New York: Oxford University Press.

Weber, Max (1921). *Economy and Society,* G. Roth and C. Wittich, eds. New York: Bedminster Press.

Whitt, J. Allen (1981). "Is oil different? A comparison of the social background and organizational affiliations of oil and non-oil directors." *Social Problems* 29:142–155.

Whitt, J. Allen (1982). *Means of Motion.* Princeton: Princeton University Press.

Zeitlin, Maurice (1974). "Corporate ownership and control: The large corporation and the capitalist class." *American Journal of Sociology* 79:1073–1119.

Zeitlin, Maurice (1980). *Classes, Class Conflict and the State.* Cambridge, Mass: Winthrop.

Winthrop.

4 Interorganizational Networks Mobilizing Action at the Metropolitan Level*

Joseph Galaskiewicz

For any political interest group to be effective at the local level, it needs to mobilize resources that will enable it to persuade or force decision makers to rule in its favor. These resources can include money and credit, expertise, good connections, jobs, legitimacy, etc. As different issues arise, different combinations of resources are needed. Laumann and Pappi (1976) envisioned these resources embodied in individual members of the local elite; Perrucci and Pilisuk (1970), Perrucci and Lewis (1984), and Turk (1973, 1977) envisioned these resources embodied in formal organizations. If the latter are correct, as issues develop, interested parties must mobilize the resources that are controlled by organizations in the community. This can be accomplished by either procuring contributions of time, money, manpower, or information from organizations; bringing organizations into a coalition; or mobilizing organizations' leaders.

The literature reviewed in this chapter suggests that the mobilization of organizational resources is dependent upon existing interorganizational networks in the community and ties between population subgroups and organizations. On the one hand, organizations that have become involved in community issues will work through their network of ties to other organizations to secure the resources they need. On the other hand, various population subgroups will mobilize organizational resources through their ties to local organizations. In either case, organizations are viewed as caches of resources that interested parties must somehow gain access to.

Organizations Mobilizing Resources through Resource Networks

A central assumption in the organizational literature is that if organizations do not have the resources they need, they will try to secure these resources from other organizations (Yuchtman and Seashore, 1967). The literature also suggests

*Funding for this research was provided by the National Science Foundation (SES 8319364), the Northwest Area Foundation, the Center for Urban and Regional Affairs (University of Minnesota), and the Program on Non-profit Organizations (Yale University).

that it will be easier to secure these resources from organizations with whom one has an ongoing relationship. That is, an organization's existing set of interorganizational ties can act as a conduit through which the resources can be secured which, in turn, enables it to achieve its goals. Although these interorganizational relationships may not have been established with this purpose in mind, they nonetheless could be useful in procuring resources (see Galaskiewicz, 1985a).

If we apply this general theory of organizational behavior to the local political arena, we would expect that organizations, when engaged in some political action, will solicit and receive politically relevant resources from those organizations with whom they have some ongoing relationship. These resources, in turn, would enable them to influence decision makers in their favor. Indeed, research has found a persisting empirical relationship between structural position in an interorganizational resource network and organizational activation and influence in different decision arenas. Based on these results, researchers have surmised that the activation, influence, or success of organizational actors was due to the resources that organizational actors secured through their interorganizational networks.

For example, Galaskiewicz (1979a, 1979b) looked at the networks of information, money, and moral support among a wide range of organizations in a town of about 32,000 (Towertown). He found that centrality in the moral support network was critical in explaining organization's activation in controversies over the elimination of a lab school-type curriculum in a local public school and the construction of a new, all-purpose health services center. Centrality in the money network was important in explaining activation in the health center issue as well. In the information network, centrality was an important predictor of activation in the school issue, a controversy over the use of excessive force to suppress student demonstrations, and a controversy over the relocation of the town's post office that had implications for downtown redevelopment. All of these effects were independent of the revenues available to the organizations, the location of their headquarters (in Towertown or elsewhere), the percentage of organizational income from local sources, and the organization's general purpose (community problem-solving, business, or community service) (Galaskiewicz, 1979a: Chapter 4).

He also found that organizations that were more central in the resource networks, or *provided* money, information, or moral support to the wealthier organizations in town, were seen by organizational elites as more influential in community affairs. However, organizations that *received* moral support from the wealthier organizations in town were more successful in getting their agenda passed in the four issues studied. Again, these effects were independent of the amount of funds and personnel available to an organization and its purpose. It is important to note that the funds available to an organization also predicted both its reputed influence and success rate across the four issues. The number of employees/volunteers affiliated with an organization was negatively related to its success rate. And, although community problem-solving organizations were more likely to be seen as influential, they were not any more successful in the four community controversies than business or community-service organizations (Galaskiewicz, 1979a: Chapter 5; 1979b).

A similar analysis was done by Knoke (1983) who studied 65 organizations and 5 general types of organizations in Indianapolis and central Indiana. Included among them were 53 social-influence associations. He also gathered data on the networks of money, information, and moral support among the organizations. He found that social-influence associations that received money, information, and support from several different sponsoring organizations (public and private) tended to be viewed by community informants as better able to "achieve their own objectives" than associations that received these resources from fewer sponsoring organizations.

What do these results tell us? Basically, we have only one major empirical finding to explain: Organizations that are more central in community-resource networks were seen by other community actors as more influential in community affairs, better able to achieve their goals, and were more likely to become activated on community issues. Centrality in a network was measured differently by Galaskiewicz and Knoke, but essentially an organization was central if it had linkages or interorganizational relationships with several other actors in the system.

To explain activation, Galaskiewicz (1979a) argued that being in the center of resource networks gave organizations access to a greater number of other organizations that could provide them with necessary resources. Because the likelihood of mobilizing resources is much greater for actors in the center of social networks, they could more confidently engage the political process. To explain the greater influence that more central actors enjoyed, Galaskiewicz (1979a) argued that decision makers and other actors in the community respected the potential of well-connected actors to establish powerful coalitions. The power of an organization is a function not simply of its own resources or control over significant events, but also of its potential to access resources of other organizations in the community. Knoke and Wood (1981) agree, arguing that central actors have the capacity to mobilize resources that other organizations control (see also Rosenthal, Fingrutd, Ethier, Karant, McDonald, 1985:1023; Aveni, 1978:189).

Knoke's (1983) explanation for the correlation between centrality and perceived influence is slightly different. Not unlike Burt (1982), Knoke views power— either potential or actual—as being directly related to structural autonomy. He argues:

> By cultivating diversified ties to large numbers of community organizations capable of supplying sustaining resources, an association's leaders can lessen the group's dependence on a single source. By spreading its needs for valued resources of money, information, and moral support among many organization sponsors, an association can better retain substantial autonomy and power to pursue its collective social influence objectives. (p. 1067)

By being central in a resource network, organizations are freed from "market constraints" and are better able to pursue their options. A reputation for being influential in community affairs or the capability to achieve its objectives simply reflects others' awareness of their autonomy.

Still, none of these studies showed that actors, which are central to interorganizational networks, actually used their interorganizational resource network to secure politically relevant resources from other organizations. We know that giving or receiving resources from other organizations enhanced an organization's reputation in the political arena, but it is not clear that these network ties ever resulted in the actual transference of politically relevant resources. For example, there is no evidence that organizations that received moral support from wealthier actors in Towertown ever received funds for some political purpose. Ideally research would document how organizations call in debts to secure the resources they need or how they get their interorganizational partners to extend them credit. Alternatively, research could show that resources obtained through network ties made some difference in the outcome of a decision. Only with this kind of data could we be sure that it was the resources obtained through the network tie and not some other factor, that made the difference in some community decision.

Organizations Mobilizing Resources through Overlapping Memberships

Another central tenet of organizational theory is that organizations will maintain a network of overlapping memberships between themselves and key organizational actors in their environment in order to extend their control over that environment (Burt, 1983). One purpose of this network is to provide information to the organization. Perrucci and Pilisuk (1970) argue that by sharing executives and directors with other organizations corporate actors can more readily access the resources of other organizations and bring them to bear in crisis situations. Organizations will try to tap into the assets of other organizations by mobilizing their own members and directors who belong to these other organizations as well.

Applying this general theory to political action at the local level, we would expect that politically active organizations would gain access to politically relevant resources through their members and directors. Organizations that have some interest in an issue outcome would mobilize the resources of other organizations by getting their own members involved in an issue. These individuals, in turn, would "drag in" or "turn on" other organizations to which they belong. These organizations would get involved in an issue as their members became more involved. In effect, organizations are using their members as a "fifth column" to enlist resources that other organizations control.

Mobilizing Organizational Leaders

Although there has been no direct test of this thesis, several studies have found that individuals who hold executive or board positions in several local organizations tend to be more active in community affairs and in policymaking circles. For example, Perrucci and Pilisuk (1970), in their study of a medium-sized Indiana town, hypothesized and found that interorganizational leaders (individuals who sat in executive or board positions of several organizations) were more likely to be identified as exercising influence in actual issues and to be viewed as having more general influence than organizational leaders (individuals who sat in executive or board positions of just one, two, or three organizations). [See also Koch and Labovitz (1976) who came up with similar results.] Those who have social control over more organizational resources through multiple organizational memberships tended to be more active and effective in different decision-making arenas.

Perrucci and Lewis (1984) returned to the same town in 1981 and replicated earlier studies (Perrucci and Pilisuk, 1970). They found basically the same empirical pattern noted earlier with basically the same organizations as nodes in the network. More interestingly, several of those individuals who were interorganizational leaders and viewed as very influential in 1969 were still in the community but were no longer interorganizational leaders and no longer seen as influential. The authors interpreted these findings as strengthening their argument that interorganizational leaders are important not because of their personalities or the resources that they control personally, but because of their positions straddling several organizations in the community simultaneously.

Although working in a somewhat different theoretical framework, Ratcliff, Gallagher, and Ratcliff (1979) and Ewen (1978) came up with similar findings. They studied the directors of 77 commercial bank boards in the St. Louis metropolitan area and examined two networks of overlapping organizational memberships: elite social clubs and the boards of the largest industrial corporations headquartered in the area. As summarized in Friedland and Palmer (1984:400), they found that:

The number of corporate board memberships a bank director possessed was highly correlated with the number of elite social clubs to which he or she belonged. More importantly, the number of each had significant, positive net effects on a director's level of participation in *policy-related groups* [italics added]. Furthermore, the centrality of a director's bank in both of these networks also influenced his or her participation. However, the attributes of the bank itself (e.g., total assets) had no net effects on the participation of its directors.

Ewen (1978) in her study of Detroit found that the 421 directors who were on the boards of the 41 largest economic enterprises tended to be well represented on the boards of Detroit cultural, civic, and business organizations. Again, those who had interorganizational power or, more specifically, were affiliated with several organizations, were more likely to be recruited to coalitions and decision-making arenas.

That interorganizational leaders were more active in community affairs is consistent with (although does not confirm) the thesis that organizational actors use their overlapping memberships to recruit other organizations to their side on some local issue. Turning again to Perrucci and Pilisuk (1970), they argue that organizations in the community are permanent figures that ensure their ability to control their environment by sharing with one another executives who can be mobilized on different issues and bring the resources of many different organizations to bear on a particular decision. As issues arise, these interorganizational agents lend support to their organizations.

Yet none of these studies documented the interests that these interorganizational leaders served. We have data on their activation and role in policy decision-making circles, but we do not know whose interests they served. Did they protect their organizations' interests in these decision contexts, or did they promote their own self-interest? Another possibility is that interorganizational leaders were simply "guns for hire." Interorganizational leaders would be attractive allies for any advocate. If an interest group could obtain their support, they might gain access to the organizational resources controlled by these leaders. That interorganizational leaders were wooed to coalitions more than organizational leaders may simply be a cost-saving strategy on the part of coalition builders. One gains access to four, five, or six organizations by getting access to one interorganizational leader. Only by looking at all participants in an issue and what is at stake can we learn if these interorganizational leaders were agents championing the cause of their respective organizations, self-serving actors, or agents of political action groups in the community.

Mobilizing Organizations

If the mobilization through overlapping memberships thesis is correct, we should also find that participation in community issues is greater among organizations in the center of these networks of overlapping memberships and that coalitional partners tend to be proximate in these networks. Laumann and Pappi's (1976) study of Altneustadt provides some of the strongest evidence that overlapping memberships are critical in explaining activation, influence, and coalition formation. They found that an organization's centrality in a network of overlapping memberships was correlated with its reputed influence in community affairs: the more central the organization, the greater its reputed influence (1976:178). Furthermore, they found that the influence ranks of organizations were directly related to their success or failure across four community issues.

Looking again at the network of overlapping memberships, Laumann and Pappi (1976:179–180) examined the positions (proponent versus opponent) of these organizations on five community issues. In general, they found that organizations that had the same position on an issue tended to be more proximate in the network of overlapping memberships. For instance, they found that the same organizations tended to be on the same side of their two pattern-maintenance issues reflecting a clear division between organizations representing Catholic and religious traditionalists from organizations representing *neubergers* and the science community. In the network of overlapping memberships, organizations representing the former were clustered together at the opposite end from organizations representing the latter. The three instrumental issues did not dissect as neatly; however, the coalitions again mirrored the structure of the network. For example, the issue of the building of a new city hall was divided precisely along the lines of political party cleavage between the Christian Democratic Union (CDU) and the German Social Democratic Party (SPD); the issue of industrial resettlement divided economic actors with large economic enterprises in opposition to small businessmen and commercial interests; and the incorporation of outlying towns into greater Altneustadt was opposed by agricultural interests whereas it was favored by the urban organizations. More important, in each case the network of overlapping memberships provided the basis upon which interest groups or coalitions were built. Opponents clustered in one region of the network, and proponents clustered in another. Coalitions might shift, depending on the issue, but cleavages still followed the structure of the network.

Whitt (1982:159–163) undertook a similar analysis of the interlocking directorates of 401 Fortune 500 and Fortune 50 firms. Using data from Sonquist and Koenig (1975:221, 224), he identified 32 cliques ranging in size from 3 to 15 firms to determine whether firms in the same cliques tended to be coalitional partners on two issues that were related to the diversion of highway trust fund monies to develop mass transit systems in California. The argument was that firms that shared directors would be recruited to the same side of a coalition. The analysis was especially provocative, because in one issue a group of firms actively opposed the diversion, while in the second another group of firms actively supported mass transit.

The results, however, ran contrary to his expectations. Among the 17 opponents to one of the propositions, there were 16 different cliques represented. Among the 28 supporters of the other proposition, there were 10 cliques represented. Also, 60% of those cliques represented by supporters of one proposition were also represented among opponents of the other, while 38% of the cliques represented in the opposition to the second proposition were represented among the supporters of the first. Clearly there was no evidence that interlocking directorates influenced the positions of firms on these issues.

In these studies as well as in those by Perrucci and Pilisuk (1970) and Perrucci and Lewis (1984; 1989) there is the nagging issue of whether those natural persons who are members of these organizations are really committed agents of their organizations. As noted earlier, these individuals could have been using their organization to further their own interests rather than acting as servants of the organization. It could also be the case that organizations are recruited to coalitions because natural persons are involved in the political process and will draw on the organizations' resources for their own purposes. Two or three organizations may support a certain proposition, not because it does them any good as organizations but because members that they share in common have an intense interest in the issue and are able to mobilize the organizations to their own ends. The key difference between this and our earlier interpretation is that before we viewed the organization as the key actor in the system, while now we are suggesting that the organization serves the interests of some constituency beyond itself.

Population Subgroups Mobilizing Resources through Overlapping Memberships

This naturally leads us to a discussion of how population subgroups gain access to organizational resources. Instead of an outright request for funding, information, or moral support, we suspect that political interest groups use their memberships in organizations to gain access to organizational resources. As we shall see, there are two studies that show that organizations with strong network ties to elite or high-status groups will expend resources in a way that clearly reflects the preferences of these outside interests. Unfortunately, since neither of these studies directly examined political action or a community decision-making event, they should be taken as illustrative only.

Ratcliff's (1980) research on the lending practices of 77 St. Louis banks clearly showed the impact of status group ties on organizational behavior. He found that commercial banks, whose directors belonged to high-status organizations or were affiliated with large corporations in the St. Louis area, tended to direct their loans to capitalist borrowers and avoid home mortgages. These effects were independent of the bank's status or size (measured in terms of deposits). Ratcliff argues that being corporate directors and members of elite organizations qualifies these men and women as members of the local capitalist class. That their banks would invest money in corporate growth indicates that control indeed has passed from bank management to the class interests represented on the boards. At this point, this class has successfully infiltrated and taken control of the organizations. Through multiple organizational members (i.e., through the creation of interorganizational ties), this class extends its control over local institutions—clubs, corporations, and financial institutions.

Galaskiewicz's (1985b) study of corporate giving demonstrated the influence of elite ties on organizational behavior as well. Looking at the contributions of 69 publicly held companies headquartered in the Minneapolis–St. Paul area from 1979 to 1981, he found that firms donated more money to charity if their chief executive officers (CEOs) were in the same social clubs or on the same prestigious boards as local philanthropic activists or if the CEOs were in the personal networks of the philanthropic activists. He also found that firms whose CEOs were proximate to the elite tended to fund those nonprofit organizations that the elite either supported or used themselves. Furthermore, those firms that contributed more money to charity were recognized by this elite as more generous and more successful business ventures. We should add that all these effects were independent of the firms' pretax net income.

In the Twin Cities case, there existed a network of semisocial ties among a group of businessmen with an elite group at the core. CEOs of different firms linked directly and indirectly to this group. In this network, the firm played two very different roles. On the one hand, it was a pawn used to further the interests of the philanthropic elite. Its contributions were influenced by its CEO being integrated into these exclusive circles and subject to peer pressure. On the other hand, the firm was the very reason that the CEO was brought into the network in the first place. Because of his position at the head of the corporation, the CEO was allowed into this elite network. Galaskiewicz (1985b) argued that membership was a function of institutional position rather than family background, social credentials, and so on. Thus, while the ties into the firm clearly influenced the contributions of companies, the firms' capacity to give influenced the potential of ties being formed between the CEOs and the elite.

Ewen (1978) also argued that ties from an interest group into local organizations furthered the interest of that elite more than the interest of the firm. In her study of 421 individuals who were directors of the 41 major economic firms headquartered in Detroit, she showed that in many cases directors of these firms (and their families) tended to be major shareholders and that directors tended to be linked through intermarriage and social ties. She then concluded that those firms whose directors were important shareholders and linked to one another socially were pawns or agents of Detroit's upper class. The organization was the agent of class interests. Unfortunately, she never offered any evidence that firms that were "pawns" behaved or acted any differently from firms that were not owner-controlled. If class is a significant variable, it should have some effect on organizational behavior.

The issue raised in this section is central to contemporary political sociology: To what extent do class interests as opposed to managerial interests dominate organizational and political decision making (see Alford and Friedland, 1985; Useem, 1984). Here the "fifth column" within the organization are agents for some class-based interest group. If one could easily identify decisions that serve managers as opposed to owners or an upper class, then researchers might begin to resolve these issues. However, it is difficult to separate out class as opposed to organizational effects empirically; likewise, it is often difficult to distinguish between managerial and class interests even analytically. Although a considerable amount of research is being done on these issues it will not be reviewed here. We only suggest that studying linkages between status groups and organizations and tying this to organizational behavior could be a fruitful way to begin to sort out these issues.

Mobilizing Coalitions through Interorganizational Organizations

At a more macrosociological level, researchers have tried to identify the structural conditions under which coalitions and problem-solving action sets emerge. Instead of focusing on the networks among organizational actors or between population subgroups and organizations and then predicting organizational activation, influence, and position on issues, analysts have tried to identify the optimal organizational conditions that give rise to coalitions and problem-solving action sets. In particular, most research has paid attention to the role played by interorganizational organizations or federations.

One of the most suggestive studies was done by Jeffrey Henig (1982) who examined mobilization efforts among neighborhood groups in six Chicago and Minneapolis neighborhoods. Henig wanted to explain why some residents were able to mount an effective response to an outside challenge to their neighborhood, while others either could not or the response was minimal and late in coming. The key variable he identified was the presence of preexisting community organizations. Henig (1982:170) found that the larger the number of organizations, the quicker the neighborhood response to a challenge; however, the number of organizations in a neighborhood did not account for the size of the mobilization efforts that eventually emerged. More important, neighborhoods that had federated community organizations (i.e., "interorganizational organizations") tended to mobilize a larger and quicker response than neighborhoods that had unitary organizations or no organizations whatsoever. Interestingly, this organizational variable seemed to be more important than the neighborhoods' demographic characteristics in explaining mobilization.

Henig's (1982) interpretation of the results is informative. First, he offers a very simple communications explanation. With the presence of interorganizational organizations, a number of key actors in the community can come to know about an outside threat in a short amount of time. This supposedly prompts a quicker response. At a more sophisticated level, he argues that the presence of some sort of federated structure provides a framework in which coalitions can be mobilized. It provides a context for potential coalitional partners to work out the old and persisting problems associated with any sort of collective action. For example, the federation can act as a "social memory" that can balance all the favors that member actors trade among themselves (see Ouchi, 1984). It will remind peers of the debts and obligations owed by different coalition partners so that others are more willing to extend credit to their neighbors knowing they will be repaid in the future. Curiously, this is the same rationalization offered by Banfield (1961) as the reason that the Chicago political machine worked—there was an accounting of who owed whom. The infrastructure ascertained that actors could be called upon to repay their debts.

In addition, a federation can provide selective incentives or sanctions to induce reluctant "free riders" to join in the collective effort. These incentives would range from minor material incentives (e.g., use of office space, typewriters, phones) to sociability goods, social status, or even ostracism from the federation. In any case, the federation exists as a pool of resources upon which collective actors could draw. The bottom line is that the federation and interorganizational relations embodied in its membership can filter resources—information, authority, or selective incentives—to emerging coalitions mobilizing for action. These federations do not themselves organize the coalition but, rather, are used by emerging community-based interests to respond to some external threat.

Herman Turk (1973, 1977) pursued a similar line of enquiry. If collective action is to take place among competing organizations within an urban community, there must be certain organizations available that facilitate coalition formation and bargaining and that can take the initiative in constructing some sort of dominant coalition to carry out policies that are agreed upon. Turk argues that the two organizations that can perform this "linking" function among formally organized interests are municipal governments and citywide consensual voluntary associations. The more these two structures can act as contact points for different interest groups in the city, the easier it will be for groups to reconcile their differences and engage in collective problem-solving.

Turk (1960), in a survey of 130 cities with populations over 100,000 in 1960, assembled a number of remarkable findings given the crudity of the variables analyzed. For example, he showed that the correlation between "need" variables (e.g., poverty or number of hospitals) and interorganizational response variables (e.g., developing a Model Cities network or establishing a hospital council) is greater in cities where city governments are larger and more diversified and where citywide consensual voluntary associations are present. Turk interprets these findings as indicating that city government and voluntary associations act as marketplaces where different demands (or interests) can be articulated, coalitions can form, and policy can be hammered out.

Working at the macrostructural level, these researchers had major measurement problems. For example, although he frequently referred to the city's interorganizational network infrastructure, Turk had no network data in his study. These are common problems at this level of analysis, yet they should not go unmentioned. Henig's (1982) problems were a little different. He created a very interesting theory that would explain the importance of interorganizational organizations, but he had no data on organization's "social memory" or even on selective incentives that these federations supposedly provided to reluctant participants. Hopefully as researchers take to the field to test these ideas, they will be sensitive to these measurement problems and gather data that can enlighten us on these issues.

Conclusion

In this last section, I would like to review what these studies can teach us. First, if we are going to focus on interorganizational relations, we must describe the actual linkages among organizations and retain the asymmetry of ties. For example, the Towertown research drew the distinction between organizations' inflows of money, information, and support and their outflows. If we found that organizations that were sources (as opposed to sinks) of money, information, and support were more influential in community affairs, we could infer that the organizations' power rests in the debts or obligations others owed them. If we found that sinks were more influential, we could infer that the continuing flow of resources to an organization was its basis of power. Our finding that reputed influence was based on outflows and success/failure across four issue areas was based on inflows does not challenge the integrity of our theory nor does it call into question our methods. It simply suggests that reputed and actual influence are based on different types of network centrality. The point is that one cannot tease out these effects without considering the direction of transactions in a network.

Second, analysts need to define and measure centrality and influence in community affairs more carefully. The strong positive correlation between these variables could be due to the fact that we have two observable indicators of one underlying latent variable instead of two genuinely distinct variables that are causally related. This is especially a problem when we use reputational measures of influence. A panel of informants could be simply using the relational position of an organizational actor as an indicator of how influential it is. If an organization is central in a network, it must be influential as well. One counterstrategy would be to use different indicators of influence. For example, Galaskiewicz (1979a) looked at organizations' "batting averages" across the four issues he studied—how many issues did organizations win and lose on—as an independent measure of political influence (see also Laumann and Pappi, 1976). Alternatively, researchers could ask organizational respondents to indicate how successful they were in achieving their goals.

Third, it is imperative that researchers incorporate all potential actors into their study of community issues. In this respect, Henig's work is a fine example. A study of just organizations (e.g., Galaskiewicz, 1979a) or just elites (Laumann, Marsden, and Galaskiewicz, 1977) or just citizen groups runs the risk of ignoring key actors in the decision-making process and misses an opportunity to more closely analyze the interface among these different social actors. For insight into how this interface might be operationalized, we should look again at the work of Laumann and Pappi (1976) who recovered the interface between their local elite and different population subgroups by asking a cross-section of community residents to describe their feelings and allegiances to members of the elite. One could recover the interface between organizations and population subgroups in like manner.

Fourth, we must remember when analyzing overlapping organizational memberships that these data can be used to recover networks both among organizations and among individuals. The theoretical implications of this duality have been discussed by Coleman (1957) and Breiger (1974). Exciting empirical work has been done by McPherson (1982). However, the most illustrative effort is still that by Perrucci and Pilisuk (1970) and Perrucci and Lewis (1984). After looking at the interorganizational network based on shared members, the authors constructed the network among interorganizational leaders based on individuals belonging to the same organizations. This reminds us that we have both an interorganizational network and a network among individuals who use the organization as an arena of interaction.

Finally, we must move beyond case studies and do more comparative research across urban systems. A major disappointment over the last 10 years is that the hypotheses developed by Herman Turk have never been retested. Several times I have alluded to the methodological weaknesses in Turk's work, but gathering the kind of network data needed to do a comprehensive comparative study is an awesome and very expensive task. Turk did the best he could with what he had. However, for this field of study to grow and develop, comparative studies across urban systems are a necessity. Only when the analyst can compare structural conditions across a variety of urban contexts can he begin to see if structure per se has any independent effect on action. By investigating only single networks, analysts have had to settle for looking at the behavior of different nodes in the network and seeing if their position within the network (or their network linkages) has any effect on if and how options are pursued. This research is necessary, but most of the new and interesting research will be done at the network level. We feel strongly that only by studying different networks and different systems can analysts address the issues that will come to bear in the years to come.

Acknowledgments

I would like to thank Ron Aminzade, David Knoke, Robert Perrucci, and Harry Potter for their useful comments on an earlier draft of this chapter.

References

Alford, Robert, and Friedland, Roger (1985). *Powers of Theory: Capitalism, the State, and Democracy*. New York: Cambridge University Press.

Aveni, Adrian F. (1978). "Organizational linkages and resource mobilization: The significance of linkage strength and breadth." *The Sociological Quarterly* 19:185–202.

Banfield, Edward (1961). *Political Influence*. New York: The Free Press.

Breiger, Ronald L. (1974). "The duality of persons and groups." *Social Forces* 53:181–190.

Burt, Ronald S. (1982). *Toward a Structural Theory of Action: Network Models of Social Structure, Perception, and Action*. New York: Academic Press.

Burt, Ronald S. (1983). *Corporate Profits and Cooptation: Networks of Market Constraints and Directorate Ties in the American Economy*. New York: Academic Press.

Coleman, James (1957). *Community Conflict*. New York: The Free Press.

Ewen, Lynda Ann (1978). *Corporate Power and Urban Crisis in Detroit*. Princeton, N.J.: Princeton University Press.

Friedland, Roger, and Palmer, Donald (1984). "Park place and main street: Business and the urban power structure." In Ralph Turner and James Short (eds.), *The Annual Review of Sociology, Vol. 10*. Palo Alto, Calif.: Annual Reviews, Inc., pp. 393–416.

Galaskiewicz, Joseph (1979). *Exchange Networks and Community Politics*. Beverly Hills: Sage. (a)

Galaskiewicz, Joseph (1979). "The structure of community organizational networks." *Social Forces* 57:1346–1364. (b)

Galaskiewicz, Joseph (1985). "Interorganizational relations." In Ralph H. Turner (ed.), *Annual Review of Sociology, Vol. II*. Palo Alto, Calif.: Annual Reviews, Inc., pp. 281–304. (a)

Galaskiewicz, Joseph (1985) *Social Organization of an Urban Grants Economy: A Study of Business Philanthropy and Nonprofit Organizations*. Orlando, Fla.: Academic Press. (b)

Henig, Jeffery R. (1982). *Neighborhood Mobilization: Redevelopment and Response*. New Brunswick, N.J.: Rutgers University Press.

Knoke, David (1983). "Organization sponsorship and influence reputation of social influence associations." *Social Forces* 61:1065–1087.

Knoke, David, and Wood, James R. (1981). *Organized for Action: Commitment in Voluntary Associations*. New Brunswick, N.J.: Rutgers University Press.

Koch, Agnes, and Labovitz, Sanford (1976). "Interorganizational power in a canadian community: A replication." *The Sociological Quarterly* 17:3–15.

Laumann, Edward, and Pappi, Franz (1976). *Networks of Collective Action: A Perspective on Community Influence Systems*. New York: Academic Press.

Laumann, Edward, Marsden, Peter, and Galaskiewicz, Joseph (1977). "Community influence structures: Replication and extension of a network approach." *American Journal of Sociology* 83:594–631.

McPherson, J. Miller (1982). "Hypernetwork sampling: Duality and differentiation among voluntary organizatins." *Social Networks* 3:225–250.

Ouchi, William G. (1984). *The M-Form Society: How American Teamwork Can Recapture the Competitive Edge*. Reading, Mass.: Addison-Wesley.

Perrucci, Robert, and Lewis, Bonnie L. (1984). "Continuity and change of interorganizational resource networks and community elite structure." Working paper, Department of Sociology and Anthropology, Purdue University.

Perrucci, Robert, and Lewis, Bonnie L. (1989). "Interorganizational relations and community influence structure: A replication and extension." *Sociological Quarterly* 30:in press.

Perrucci, Robert, and Pilisuk, Marc (1970). "Leaders and ruling elites: The interorganizational bases of community power." *American Sociological Review* 35:1040–1057.

Ratcliff, Richard E. (1980). "Capitalist class impact on lending behavior of banks." *American Sociological Review* 45:553–570.

Ratcliff, Richard E., Gallagher, Mary Elizabeth, and Ratcliff, Kathryn Strother (1979). "The civic involvement of bankers: An analysis of the influence of economic power and social prominence in the command of civic policy positions." *Social Problems* 26:298–313.

Rosenthal, Naomi, Fingrutd, Meryl, Ethier, Michelle, Karant, Roberta, and McDonald, David (1985). "Social movements and network analysis: A case study of nineteenth-century women's reform in New York State." *American Journal of Sociology* 90:1022–1054.

Sonquist, John A., and Koenig, Thomas (1975). "Interlocking directorates in the top U.S. corporations: A graph theory approach." *Insurgent Sociologist* 5:196–229.

Turk, Herman (1973). *Interorganizational Activation in Urban Communities: Deductions from the Concept of Systems*. Washington, D.C.: The Arnold and Caroline Rose Monograph Series, American Sociological Association.

Turk, H. (1977). *Organizations in Modern Life*. San Francisco: Jossey-Bass.

Useem, Michael (1984). *The Inner Circle: Large Corporations and the Rise of Business Political Activity in the U.S. and U.K.* New York: Oxford University Press.

Whitt, J. Allen (1982). *Urban Elites and Mass Transportation*. Princeton, N.J.: Princeton University Press.

Yuchtman, Ephraim, and Seashore, Stanley (1967). "A systems resource approach to organizational effectiveness." *American Sociological Review* 32:891–903.

5 Organizational Ties and Urban Growth

J. Allen Whitt

My purpose in this chapter is to suggest ways in which the study of interorganizational relations can contribute to our understanding of the nature of cities, the processes of urban development, and the exercise of local political power.

The literatures on cities, urban development, and urban politics are vast, and the interorganizational relations literature is extensive. My topic is delimited by focusing upon certain important perspectives and research traditions that have been developing during the last 10–15 years. I will concentrate on two areas: (1) the urban "growth machine" thesis, and (2) that branch of interorganizational studies known as network analysis, especially as it relates to the study of urban power and influence structures. Some of these developments will be briefly and selectively summarized, how they converge within urban sociology will be highlighted, and some possible new directions for future research will be sketched out.

The Growth Machine Thesis

In 1976 Harvey Molotch published "The City as a Growth Machine." Significantly, the subtitle of that article was "Toward a Political Economy of Place." It was an attempt to link the political, the economic, and the spatial all in one notion of urban growth and development. The piece attracted a lot of attention within urban sociology circles and became the basis for an influential and continuing research tradition.

In essence, Molotch's argument is that a city may be thought of as a geographic location in which the land-based interests of an elite are given expression. The city is an aggregate of parcels of land, a mosaic, with each parcel representing a landowner or other interested individual who "has in mind a certain future for that parcel which is linked somehow with his or her own well-being" (Molotch, 1976:310). Well-being, at least for commercial interests, is typically pursued through trying to enhance the profit-making potential of the land. This often means that landowners want to see development, growth, and increasing intensity of land use on their parcel and on those parcels that surround it: The restaurant owner wants more business and a bigger operation; the banker wants to get more deposits and make more loans; the developer wants to tear down the old bowling alley and put up condominiums; the shop keeper wants to see the new urban transportation center located across the street from her business; the local newspaper publisher wants to have more readers and to sell more lines of ads. Since the fate of one's own property is affected by what uses adjacent parcels are put to, both conflict and cooperation arise among land-based elites. Sometimes growth is a zero-sum game in which one's gains are at the expense of one's neighbor. There may be conflict over where to locate the new shopping center or the city garbage dump. On the other hand, there may be cooperation: Just about all landowners may agree that it would be to their benefit if a new research and development facility moved *somewhere* into the city, and, thus, they may all join to lobby for that outcome. As interests are connected, there is also a collective interest in generating overall growth in the area, not just on individual parcels of land. The city thus becomes "a mosaic of competing land interests capable of strategic coalition and action" (Molotch, 1976:311).

One of the prime activities of growth coalitions, according to the Molotch analysis, is the attempt to organize local political and economic resources in such a manner as to make the city an attractive location for the in-migration of outside businesses and mobile capital. In this effort, government activities are crucial, as are decisions made by large landowners and employers, such as major corporations. Local and state governments and corporations are lobbied by the local growth coalition in an attempt to generate the infrastructural preconditions (e.g., tax concessions, vocational training, new sewer service extensions) and private capital investments thought necessary for future growth in the area. Thus, cities become "growth machines," always in competition with other cities for the limited national pool of growth and capital and always striving toward more extensive and intensive patterns of local land use.

Molotch remarks that urban growth is, in part, the result of an exercise of political *power* and not simply the result of inevitable subsocial ecological or economic forces that transcend any single locality. The thesis also points out that, to a significant extent, growth may be a *zero-sum game,* both from the standpoint of the various groups that inhabit one city and from the standpoint of one city versus another. What is beneficial and profitable to the growth coalition—the businesses, commercial landowners, "rentiers" (Molotch, 1979) and others—may not be in the interests of residents and those of lesser power who use the city as a place to live: Taxes may go up, schools and community facilities may become overcrowded, the stability and quality of neighborhoods may decline, traffic may become more oppressive, air and water quality may suffer, etc. The struggle for growth often pits one city against another, resulting in what may be for each city a ruinous competition of tax concessions, construction of industrial parks and job training facilities at public expense, softening of pollution control regulations, and the like, in what may be unsuccessful attempts to attract footloose industries and capital investment into the area (see, e.g., Bluestone and Harrison, 1982).

Growth politics operates at both the individual level—for example, the decision of a landowner to construct an office tower—and the collective level—for example, the banding together of downtown businesses to lobby city government to grant tax concessions or to create urban enterprise zones. Government institutions play a crucial role in the politics of growth, leading Molotch to assert that "this organized effort to affect the outcome of growth distribution is the essence of local government as a dynamic political force" (Molotch, 1976:313). The study of the political–economic processes of growth and the structure and operation of the network of organizations that implements growth policies are phenomena that deserve to be at the center of the urban research agenda.

Certainly, previous studies of community power and urban politics have examined issues that are relevant to urban growth: for example, whether a new convention center will be built and, if so, where; the nature and extent of downtown urban renewal programs. These studies contribute to our grasp of the politics of growth. Yet, what the growth machine perspective adds is the notion of urban growth politics as an issue *area* that may be able to give a degree of unity to the interests of local land-based elites over time and over a range of specific growth-relevant issues. Studies of growth politics may thus tell us much about the extent and limits of elite dominance and unity, a topic of considerable importance and controversy.

Network Analysis

Molotch (1976) argues that in order to try to secure to themselves the benefits of growth, progrowth forces attempt to make coalitions with others of similar inclination—this, in fact, becomes the basis of "community" for them—and together they press the local government to create the basic conditions favorable to urban growth. If true, one would expect to find interorganizational networks among progrowth forces and between these forces and public agencies—networks that fuel the political engines of growth at the local level.

Although this field of inquiry is still largely nascent, there is a growing literature that will become increasingly crucial in our comprehension of urban growth and urban politics. Of relevance are not only earlier studies of "civic boosterism" by local movers and shakers, and the extensive "community power" literature, but also recent studies that (1) recognize the political economics of urban growth as fundamental and (2) analyze interorganizational networks in order to examine the local structure of growth-inducing politics. This recent work builds upon previous urban and political literatures as well as upon the current literature on corporate actors, urban networks, and interlocking director-ates (e.g., Mintz and Schwartz, 1981; Laumann, Marsden, and Galaskiewicz, 1977; Laumann and Marsden, 1979; Sonquist and Koenig, 1975; Mizruchi, 1982).

Perrucci and Pilisuk (1970) argue that interorganizational networks are an essential ingredient for the collective exercise of power because they permit the pooling of necessary resources. The research findings of their 1970 study indicate that leaders who head interorganizational networks not only have a reputation for power, but also exhibit disproportionate participation in local issues, have greater value homophyly [1], and see each other socially. Whitt and Mizruchi (1986) find that local interorganizational leaders have greater objective knowledge concerning national level elite business organizations, suggesting that these leaders are less parochial in their orientation (cf. Useem, 1984), and that they participate in communication channels and political linkages that tie localities to the national scene. In a replication of the 1970 study, Perrucci and Lewis (1984) show that there is a great deal of stability in networks over time—in this case a period of 13 years.

The work of Ratcliff, Oehler, and Gallops (1979b) and Ratcliff (1980a, b) demonstrates that the structure of intercorporate relations affects the loan policies of banks. Banks having extensive interlocks with other corporations and with elite social circles tend to put more money into capital loans to businesses and less into home mortgage loans. Since capital loans are a crucial resource for business expansion and urban development, this work suggests one system of growth-relevant connections, that is, a financial pipeline between banks and other lending firms and commercial businesses and developers.

This work also implies that the distribution of intracity capital resources will be highly unequal, both among businesses and for residences vis-à-vis businesses. However, the policies of major banks may be contradictory. While bankers are closely tied to the leading economic, social, and civic circles in their localities, their banks make a disproportionate amount of loans to large corporations, the very organizations that are most likely national or international in their operations. This may result in an outflow from the metropolitan area of capital that could be used for local development purposes. As Ratcliff puts it: "The leading St. Louis capitalists appear to be playing complex and even contradictory roles . . . [reflecting] the dual needs . . . to protect both their local class bases and their long-term interests by taking advantage of national economic trends" (1980b:568). In analyzing the politics of urban growth and decline, it is crucial to understand the relation between banks and elite social circles and the various firms and sectors of the local economy.

In an earlier work, I suggest the relevance of intercorporate connections for analyzing the politics of urban growth in California (Whitt, 1982). The Bay Area

Rapid Transit (BART) system was viewed by the corporate community primarily as a means of inducing centralized growth in downtown San Francisco and only secondarily as a system of people transport. BART was promoted and strongly supported by an integrated network of big businesses that centered on the Bay Area Council. Consistent with the findings of Perrucci and Pilisuk (1970) and Perrucci and Lewis (1984), the Bay Area Council was more a network of specific firms than of individuals (Whitt, 1982:43), implying the existence of a stable interorganizational network strongly devoted to influencing urban growth politics in the area.

The politics of growth in the BART case was complex. Interorganizational analysis helps us to comprehend the complexity. As Molotch argues, growth politics may involve both cooperation and conflict among progrowth forces (Molotch, 1976:311; Molotch and Logan, 1984). In the case of BART, there was both consensus and potential conflict among the supporters of BART. While large San Francisco-based corporations appeared to agree that BART was a good thing and thus gave organizational and financial support to its campaign, there was also a group of companies, the so-called "highway lobby," that was opposed to using part of the highway fund to pay for its construction. These firms were not opposed to the generation of urban growth, nor even to the construction of a mass transit system per se, but they did engage in a struggle over the source of capital to finance the system. In this struggle, connections among companies and between firms and other organizations (e.g., bank clearing houses, political campaign organizations, and trade associations) played instructive, if complex, roles (Whitt, 1982).

Recent work by Shlay and Giloth (1985) also uses interorganizational data to help understand another form of urban growth politics: the attempt to stage a World's Fair in Chicago in 1992. World's Fairs are typically heavily subsidized by public monies and result in massive downtown expansion and redevelopment of the cities in which they are held. As the authors state: "World's Fairs have gone further than urban renewal clearance; they have enabled land acquisition and clearance, have built commercial structures, convention centers, opera houses, and hotels, and have created parks, landscaping and improved downtown highway nexus" (Shlay and Giloth, 1985:6).

The planning for the proposed 1992 Chicago fair was carried out by a nonprofit organization, the 1992 Corporation. Analysis demonstrates that this organization was embedded in an extensive and tightly knit network of the largest corporations, banks, planning organizations, civic organizations, and exclusive social clubs in the Chicago area. For example, the 17 firms that were most tightly connected to the 1992 Corporation (through having at least two of the firm's employees as members of the 1992 Corporation) "brought to the 1992 Corporation a web of 186 separate interlocks with themselves and with other World's Fair firms" (Shlay and Giloth, 1985:16–17).

Shlay and Giloth (1985:23) conclude that "shared interests, a tight network, and direct connections to Chicago's corporate, financial and civic organizational structures put the 1992 Fair on the public's agenda, not a set of innovative ideas." This was possible because the movers and shakers had been organized ahead of time by mutual affiliations and concerns and had an effective political and organizational structure in place into which the World's Fair issue could be injected.

Yet, despite the existence of a tight interorganizational network, ultimate success in bringing about specific, urban progrowth policies is not always assured. The World's Fair will not be held in Chicago—at least not in 1992. Although the advocacy groups mentioned previously are still trying to revive the plans for the fair, such factors as the lackluster performance of recent fairs, accelerating costs, and increased public opposition led to a cut-off of public funding by the Illinois legislature in 1985 (Shlay and Giloth, 1985:4).

As the cases of San Francisco BART and the Chicago World's Fair remind us, despite the political cohesion that the overall goal of urban growth may inspire, progrowth policies may be complex in their effects and do not automatically generate unity among residents or even among business and development interests. There may be opposition from citizen's groups, disagreements among growth advocates over specific plans, fragmentation between business and political leaders, or a changing economic and political environment that alters the calculus of the interested parties as growth plans develop. For example, Bennett, McCourt, Nyden, and Squires (1987) argue that while Chicago politics overall approximates the growth machine model, specific projects such as the North Loop redevelopment project sometimes run into difficulties due to opposition by neighborhood groups, historic preservationists, politicians who have an independent political base in party machines and are thus not directly beholden to development interests, and to disagreements between developers and other businesses over particulars of the plan. Molotch (1976) notes that growth interests and coalitions exist in a geographically nested fashion, with cooperation at one level possibly becoming conflict at another level. For instance, while the entire local business community may agree that a new shopping mall would be a good thing for the city, they may disagree—given their own self-interested calculations of associated economic spill-over effects—about just where such a mall should be constructed. There may also be conflicts between nationally oriented capital and local rentiers. Logan and Molotch (1986) argue that due to the increasing concentration of capital in the hands of large national and multinational firms, "local branch operations of large corporations are less useful to the local growth machines than indigenous firms used to be (p. 203)." Rentiers are sometimes less enthusiastic about such plants, since it is increasingly recognized that personnel recruitment is often from within the company instead of from the community, that raw materials and producer services are often drawn from other branches of the corporation or from other sources outside the community, and that branch plants "tend to function as economically isolated business activities, failing to stimulate growth in other local economic sectors" (1986:203).

Despite the disagreements that growth politics may induce, the desire for growth typically is a powerful unifying force among the members of the growth coalition, and various growth strategies are vigorously pursued. Even strategies not usually thought of as relevant to urban growth may be used. Within recent years, growth coalitions in many American cities have seized upon the performing arts as a means of spurring downtown growth and redevelopment (Whitt, 1987). Given that the audience for the traditional so-called "high arts" (ballet, opera, orchestra, theater) tends to come overwhelmingly from the upper socioeconomic groups (Dimaggio and Useem, 1978:187–191), the arts increasingly are viewed as useful tools in transforming central areas into more attractive locations for the managerial, professional, and white-collar workers of growing urban service economies. Recently constructed arts facilities are often contained in multiple-use developments (MXDs) that generate what developers call "market synergy" by attracting the more affluent consumers into the central city after normal working hours. In the words of one New York City theater-district developer: "We find that actors walking around the streets, theater activities in general, give off good vibrations; they make an area more renewable. If cement factories did that, we would be putting them in" (quoted in Clack, 1983:13).

Downtown arts facilities represent a publicly and privately subsidized form of land clearance, physical structure development, and historic preservation, which, as of yet, is largely noncontroversial and lacks effective political opposition. Public and private subsidies to arts groups, in the form of corporate, foundation, and public grants and contributions, have greatly increased over the last 20 years. The reasons for corporate giving are no doubt complex and difficult to specify. In his large-scale study of corporate philanthropy in one metropolitan area, Galaskiewicz (1985:90) finds that the reasons for donating (to philanthropic causes in general, not just the arts) advanced most frequently by firms themselves include: civic duty/social responsibility to the community; public relations for the company; promoting general benefits for the business community; and improving relations with employees, customers, and business peers [2]. DiMaggio and Useem (1982) argue that the increase in corporate contributions to the arts has been associated with an historical shift from "elite control" to "corporate control" of arts organizations. While elite board members were more concerned with using the high arts as a "screening" device to mark upper class boundaries and as a "yardstick for assessing the merit and cultivation of persons," the rise of corporate-dominated arts boards has resulted in more emphasis on the "legitimating" functions of arts patronage, conveying an image of contributing firms as civic-minded and respectable. The findings of Burt

(1982) are compatible with both those of Galaskiewicz and of DiMaggio and Useem. He argues that corporate philanthropy is an attempt, as is advertising, to coopt consumers. "Corporate philanthropy can both legitimate the firm to the public as a protector of the public interest . . . and provide a further stimulus to demand [for the goods produced by the firm]" (Burt, 1983:441). In still other cases, the chief executive officer of a corporation may have a personal interest in one or more of the arts and will therefore use his or her authority to influence the firm's pattern of contributions.

Thus my argument is not that the desire to stimulate downtown growth and redevelopment is the sole motivation for increased public and private support for the arts. Yet it appears to be one important motivation. Corporations and business people are typically quite interested in urban growth and redevelopment, especially in downtown areas. In his study of Atlanta, for instance, Stone (1976:38) observes that the goal of urban growth is "the glue that has held the Atlanta business community together as a political force." Businesses have recognized that the arts have growth- and redevelopment-inducing features, as outlined earlier. During the planning stages for the Kentucky Center for the Arts in Louisville, for example, a local corporate fund drive was launched that was said to "include every important name in Louisville business" (Yater, 1983). At this preliminary stage in the analysis of current Louisville data on contributions to the arts, there appear to be quite direct links between giving to the arts and promoting downtown development. In essence, the same firms that contribute heavily to the arts, and are frequently on the governing boards of arts organizations, are also strongly represented on the boards of private organizations that support urban growth and downtown redevelopment [3]. Banks appear to be particularly well represented in this network. This finding lends support to the work of Ratcliff, Gallagher, and Ratcliff (1979a:304–306) who demonstrate that the directors of the largest St. Louis banks are heavily represented on both the Arts and Education Council, which raises funds for arts groups, and the Regional Commerce and Growth Association, which has been leading business efforts in trying to stimulate the "rebirth" of downtown St. Louis.

Needs for Future Research

The literature cited here represents an important beginning toward understanding the complexities of the politics of urban growth. Many questions remain unanswered, and much theoretical and empirical work remains to be done. I will end by suggesting a sample agenda for future research and theoretical refinement.

The greatest need is to systematically combine the techniques of network analysis to research questions suggested by the growth machine thesis. Using the techniques of network analysis, it should be possible to identify the organizational channels and connections that operate to further the collective aspect of the politics of urban growth and to resolve potential and real conflicts among growth coalition members. In this latter respect, we have to be mindful of the need to identify preferences, not just formal links (Laumann and Marsden, 1979:730). Field work and interviews designed to uncover intentions are needed in addition to the abstract examination of networks. What are the interests and preferences and the oppositional structures that may arise to resist growth or resist specific forms of growth (cf. Molotch and Logan, 1984)? How consistently over time are urban elites united on growth-relevant issues? How often do policy outcomes favor progrowth forces? Some landowners and businesses have a greater ability to "exit" the local area than do others (Friedland and Palmer, 1984). What difference does this factor make in their willingness to take active roles in local growth politics? For example, does the lack of geographic mobility of banks bring them into the center of local growth politics? Pluralists and some structural Marxists argue that business elites are often fragmented and in disagreement on issues of social policy. Do these elites typically care more about the urban growth issue than they do about other issues such as, say, abortion or welfare expenditures, and is the growth issue able, as the growth machine model suggests, to inspire a greater degree of overall elite unity than the pluralist model would imply? Indeed, the question of the salience to elites of various political policies has been one upon which many criticisms of pluralist theory have been founded. Is there a particular salience and unity-inducing character in the issue of growth?

Can network analysis help us to understand to what extent local elites are able, vis-à-vis regional and national economic forces, to cause overall growth to take place in their city? Does the web of organizational ties between local areas and higher levels of economic and governmental power (e.g., local elites' member-ships in the Business Council or in top-level governmental commissions) affect the growth fortunes of localities? Is there a special growth-related role played by the "inner circle" of corporate leaders at the national (Useem, 1984) or local levels (Whitt and Mizruchi, 1986)? We need to be mindful also that the politics of growth and the structure of local networks will likely depend upon such factors as the size of the city, the nature of the local economy, the degree of economic and social differentiation of the area, the extent to which social as opposed to professional or business ties are used to reduce communication distance (Laumann *et al.*, 1977), and so on.

Not all issues relating to growth may be discoverable by interorganizational analysis, of course. The growth machine perspective suggests that both "instru-mental" aspects—that is, that organized interests will aim to attain concentrated, specific benefits for themselves—and "symbolic" aspects—attempts will be made to persuade voters and citizens that growth will bring added jobs, a promise often unfilled (Molotch, 1976)—of the politics of growth will exist (Edelman,

1967). It is the former that are particularly amenable to organizational analysis. Finally, to the extent that progrowth policies are a taken-for-granted reality and a source of background assumptions for local political and economic elites, they may also form the basis for what Bachrach and Baratz (1962) have called the "second face of power," the hidden face that is not discoverable simply by the analysis of concrete decisions. While such possible "nondecisions" may escape analyses that rely upon the activation of networks on specific policy decisions, the identification of a growth bias may add to our understanding of what kinds of issues may be organized *out* of politics (e.g., Crenson, 1971). The goal of urban growth essentially may serve to rule out consideration and discussion of alternative policies aimed at controlling growth.

In short, the case presented here has been that the urban growth perspective can be combined with network and interorganizational analytical techniques to provide an important research agenda filled with unanswered questions. Such an approach holds as its main promise the understanding of the *political* and *social* dimensions of urban growth. Too often, the processes of urban growth are seen as determined by purely *economic* forces—all-powerful, ineluctable, subsocial forces that operate much like the laws of gravity. In his influential book, for example, political scientist Paul Peterson (1981) applauds local growth booster-ism, arguing that local urban growth and development is to the "benefit of all residents," (1981:21) rather than specific groups, and that cities are compelled by external market forces to pursue growth aggressively. Such a view leaves little or no room for political and social factors to influence the process, since, in Peterson's view, any locally instituted policies that stand in the way of growth—as, for instance, redistributive measures—will not be instituted since presumably they damage the interests of all residents. To Peterson, therefore, the costs of growth and the political and social forces that generate and shape growth are of little scholarly or practical concern. Not surprisingly, other scholars, including political scientists, have challenged this essentially apolitical and economically deterministic perspective on urban growth (see, e.g., Swanstrom, 1986, 1987; Reed, 1986), and sociologists have been developing political–economic–social arguments based upon conceptions of growth machines, net-works of urban political power, and inner circles. These developments signal a growing realization of the inadequacies of purely economic models of urban development and point toward the continuing productive evolution of the analysis of the political and social aspects of urban growth. In this, interorganiza-tional and network studies should have a fundamental part to play.

Notes

1. The issue of value homophyly is unsettled, however. Koch and Labovitz (1976) were not able to replicate the findings of Perrucci and Pilisuk (1970)

regarding homophyly. More recently, Perrucci and Lewis (1989), in a 1981 replication of their own work, found that interorganizational leaders (IOLs) were more likely than persons with fewer organizational connections to exhibit homophyly, but the IOLs in 1981 did not exhibit so high a degree of homophyly as had IOLs in the 1969 study. Useem (1978), in a national sample of business executives holding multiple and single directorships, found neither greater homophyly for multiple directors nor differences in political attitudes between the two groups. Whitt and Mizruchi (1986), in a study of Louisville, found only weak support for the homophyly thesis.

2. Of course, the desire to stimulate urban growth would no doubt be seen by firms as benefitting the business community or the larger community.

3. For example, one of the most important ties between the corporate world and local arts development involves Humana, Inc., a company that has recently been making headlines with the artificial heart operations that it has sponsored. Humana, the second-largest hospital management firm in the country, has located its new national headquarters (filled with expensive corporate art) just across the street from the Kentucky Center for the Arts. In addition, a top officer of Humana now serves as the chairman of the governing body of the Center, was central in the supervision of the planning and construction of the Center, and has given much personal and corporate financial support to the Center and to other arts organizations in town.

References

Bachrach, Peter, and Baratz, Morton (1962). "Two faces of power." *American Political Science Review* 57:947–952.

Bennett, Larry, McCourt, K., Nyden, P., and Squires, G. (1987). "Chicago's North Loop redevelopment project: Growth machine on hold." In Scott Cummings (ed.), *Business Elites and Urban Development*. New York: State University of New York Press.

Bluestone, Barry, and Harrison, Bennett (1982). *The Deindustrialization of America*. New York: Basic Books.

Burt, Ronald (1983). "Corporate philanthropy as a cooptive relation." *Social Forces* 62:419–449.

Clack, George (1983). "Footlight districts." In K. Green (ed.), *The City as a Stage: Strategies for the Arts in Urban Economics*. Washington, D.C.: Partners for Livable Places, pp. 12–15.

Crenson, Matthew (1971). *The Un-Politics of Air Pollution: A Study of Non-Decision-making in the Cities*. Baltimore: Johns Hopkins University Press.

DiMaggio, Paul, and Useem, Michael (1978). "Cultural democracy in a period of cultural expansion: The social composition of arts audiences in the United States." *Social Problems* 26:179–197.

DiMaggio, Paul, and Useem, Michael (1982). "The Arts in Class Reproduction." In M. Apple (ed.), *Cultural and Economic Reproduction in Education*. New York: Methuen, pp. 181–201.

Edelman, Murray (1967). *The Symbolic Uses of Politics*. Chicago: University of Illinois Press.

Friedland, Roger, and Palmer, Donald (1984). "Park Place and Main Street: Business and the urban power structure." *Annual Review of Sociology* 10:393–416.

Galaskiewicz, Joseph (1985). *Social Organization of an Urban Grants Economy*. New York: Academic Press.

Koch, A., and Labovitz, S. (1976). "Interorganizational power in a Canadian community: A replication." *Sociological Quarterly* 17:3–15.

Laumann, Edward, and Marsden, Peter (1979). "The analysis of oppositional structures in political elites: Identifying collective actors." *American Sociological Review* 44: 713–732.

Laumann, Edward, Marsden, P., and Galaskiewicz, J. (1977). "Community-elite influence structures: Extension of network approach." *American Journal of Sociology* 83:594–631.

Logan, John, and Molotch, Harvey (1986). *Urban Fortunes: The Political Economy of Place*. Berkeley, Calif.: University of California Press.

Mintz, Beth, and Schwartz, Michael (1981). "Interlocking directorates and interest group formation." *American Sociological Review* 46(6):851–869.

Mizruchi, Mark (1982). *The Structure of the American Intercorporate Network, 1904–1974*. New York: Sage.

Molotch, Harvey (1976). "The city as a growth machine: Toward a political economy of place." *American Journal of Sociology* 82:309–331.

Molotch, Harvey (1979). "Capital and neighborhood in the United States." *Urban Affairs Quarterly* 14:289–312.

Molotch, Harvey, and Logan, John (1984). "Tensions in the growth machine: Overcoming resistance to value-free development." *Social Problems* 31:483–499.

Perrucci, Robert, and Lewis, Bonnie (1984). "Continuity and change of interorganizational resource networks and community elite structure." Unpublished paper, Department of Sociology, Purdue University.

Perrucci, Robert, and Lewis, Bonnie L. (1989). "Interorganizational Relations and Community Influence Structure: A Replication and Extension." *Sociological Quarterly* 30:in press.

Perrucci, Robert, and Pilisuk, Marc (1970). "Leaders and ruling elites: The interorganizational bases of community power." *American Sociological Review* 35:1040–1057.

Peterson, Paul (1981). *City Limits*. University of Chicago Press.

Ratcliff, Richard (1980). "Banks and the command of capital flows: An analysis of capitalist class structure and mortgage disinvestment in a metropolitan area." In Maurice Zeitlin (ed.), *Classes, Class Conflict, and the State*. Cambridge, Mass.: Winthrop. (a)

Ratcliff, Richard (1980). "Banks and corporate lending: An analysis of the impact of the internal structure of the capitalist class on the lending behavior of banks." *American Sociological Review* 45:553–570. (b)

Ratcliff, Richard, Gallagher, M., and Ratcliff, K. (1979). "The civic involvement of bankers: An analysis of the influence of economic power and social prominence in the command of civic policy positions." *Social Problems* 26:298–313. (a)

Ratcliff, Richard, Oehler, K., and Gallops, M. (1979). "Networks of financial power: An analysis of the impact of the internal structure of the capitalist class on the lending behavior of banks." Presented at the annual meeting of the American Sociologial Association, Boston. (b)

Reed, Adolph (1986). "A critique of neo-progressive theorizing about local development policy: A case from Atlanta." Presented at the annual meeting of the American Political Science Association, Washington, D.C.

Shlay, Anne, and Giloth, Robert (1985). "The social organization of a land based elite: Promoters of the 1992 World's Fair." Presented at the annual meeting of the American Sociological Association, Washington, D.C.

Sonquist, John, and Koenig, Thomas (1975). "Interlocking directorates in the top U.S. firms." *Insurgent Sociologist* 5:196–229.

Stone, Clarence (1976). *Economic Growth and Neighborhood Discontent.* Chapel Hill, N.C.: University of North Carolina Press.

Swanstrom, Todd (1986). "Semisovereign cities: The political logic of urban development." Presented at the annual meeting of the American Political Science Association, Washington, D.C.

Swanstrom, Todd (1987). "Urban populism, uneven development, and the space for reform." In Scott Cummings (ed.), *Business Elites and Urban Development.* New York: State University of New York Press.

Useem, Michael (1978). "The inner group of the American capitalist class." *Social Problems* 25:225–40.

Useem, Michael (1984). *The Inner Circle: Large Corporations and the Rise of Business Political Activity in the U.S. and U.K.* New York: Oxford University Press.

Whitt, J. Allen (1982). *Urban Elites and Mass Transportation: The Dialectics of Power.* Princeton, N.J.: Princeton University Press.

Whitt, J. Allen (1987). "Mozart in the metroplis: The arts coalition and the urban growth machine." *Urban Affairs Quarterly* 23:15–36.

Whitt, J. Allen, and Mizruchi, Mark (1986). "The local inner circle." *Journal of Political and Military Sociology* 14:115–125.

Yater, George (1983). "Kentucky Center for the Arts: A 17-year production." *Louisville Magazine* (November):17–26.

6 Network Perspectives and Policy Analysis: A Skeptical View

David A. Caputo

From the political scientist's vantage point, the study of decision making utilizing interorganizational analysis is both promising and frustrating. In many respects, the problems associated with prior community decision-making analysis abound, yet those who use the interorganizational approach clearly offer a variety of innovative efforts to deal with the basic conceptual and methodological problems that have long plagued the decision-making literature.

Perhaps the most perplexing problem limiting interorganizational analysis is the definition of "power" and how it is exercised. In order to make a convincing argument, it is imperative that power be clearly defined and examples of its use clearly delineated. As the dispute between the "elitists" and "pluralists" of the 1960s indicated (Hawley and Wirt, 1974), there is often little common ground for agreement when sociologists and political scientists study the same decision-making process.

The problems remain in the 1980s: How is power to be defined and how does one measure it? The political scientist is likely to argue for specific analysis of overt decision making, while the sociologist is more likely to stress the questions that are not asked or raised by the political system's participants. In addition, when studying the same decision or the same decision-making process, the political scientist and the sociologist are likely to use different methods and draw different conclusions from the same observations. For instance, if only members of upper income groups participate in a decision, the sociologist is more likely to assume the outcome of that decision benefits those participating than the political scientist who would ask for an analysis of that decision and the specific impact it has.

Perhaps the problem is even more basic than I have just described it. It may be a matter of one's worldview—the sociologist is more likely to see all society organized in an hierarchical fashion with the decisions by the few at the top levels of society influencing the many with the added assumption that the influence is negative. For the political scientist, this would be a set of questions to be investigated, not assumed. This schism clearly has an impact on any analysis, including mine, of ways to study decision making and the policymaking process. Rather than dismissing the arguments that preceded this chapter, it is useful to assess the specific strengths and weaknesses of the interorganizational analysis approach and evaluate what it offers to increase our understanding of the policy process.

Interorganizational analysis is important since it views power residing in organizations rather than individual actors and concentrates its analysis on the organizations involved in the decision-making process. Thus the composition of the organization, how it participates in the policy process, and the outcome of that process become the critical variables. The emphasis is on associating organizational participation with specific policy outcomes.

The approach involves a variety of empirical methods—from aggregate data analysis to participant observation—with the goal of attempting to explain how decisions are reached within the context of the organizational structure and interaction. Desired policy outcomes are examined and resulting policy decisions are examined to see how close they come to the desired outcomes. As Robert Spitzer (1987:674) has argued, "theory building, whether in the realm of policy studies or elsewhere, often incorporates an ad hoc admixture of deductive and inductive explorations." Interorganizational analysis relies on this theoretical basis for its explanatory power. It is a different way of not only undertaking research, but of viewing empirical reality.

Many of the issues raised by Hawley and Wirt (1974) in their *The Search for Community Power* are relevant to any discussion of interorganizational analysis. In fact, a review of that literature and the debate over various issues is a most useful way to understand many of the strengths of interorganizational analysis. Unfortunately this approach is not without dangers, and many of these remind one of the debate of the 1960s. For instance, can one conclude, as is often the case, that the leadership of an organization reflects the organization's membership as well as its underlying values?

We know that organizational leadership is not always representative of the organizational membership, and this makes it difficult to understand why a set of policies may be pursued or are deemed desirable. It is the absence of a specific linkage between membership and leadership that makes this type of analysis so difficult and sometimes impossible to do. How does one account for this discrepancy—few do. Even more difficult is the basic question in the analysis of decision making: What constitutes the use of power and what does not? Just because a particular policy preference is held by a particular group does not mean that the group has "won" if their position becomes formal policy. It is this element of causality that is at the center of the problem. How can one prove that action A led to action B? Here the contextual analysis offered by the interorganizational approach is critical. As the earlier chapters have indicated, the analysis provides the basis for a series of important conclusions about the policymaking processes in the respective communities, but is the analysis correct?

Can one assume, without a clearly defined view of power, that the empirical observations are linked to power relationships or are the observations simply a set of impressions based on association and interaction that may have little or nothing to do with power?

One final point needs to be raised. Interorganizational analysis becomes most useful when it is seen as one of a variety of methodological approaches to understanding the policymaking process rather than when it is seen as the only way to understand the policymaking process. Interorganizational analysis, properly done, adds to our understanding of decision making because it focuses on a different set of participants and perhaps even a different part of the decision-making process than do the other more traditional approaches. The traditional approaches tend to focus on institutions and individuals and how they interact at specific points in the decision-making process. Patricia Ingraham (1987) has argued that this approach too often ignored policy design and maintains that a full concentration on policy design would make "subsequent policy processes and analyses . . . clear" (p. 624). Note the emphasis on process rather than outcome—clearly a major difference between the different disciplines. With these points in mind, a brief discussion of each paper is in order.

I'll begin with Joseph Galaskiewicz's chapter on networks mobilizing action at the metropolitan level (Chapter 4). Three general points need to be raised. First, it is not clear to me to what these organizations are responding. We are told it is the general economic recession and not specific budget cuts, but evidence to support this includes statewide unemployment rates and not city or neighborhood unemployment figures.

There is no direct evidence linking high unemployment and organizational behavior? Should there be? I would think so. Perhaps an example helps to illustrate my point. There is high unemployment in Minnesota's Iron Range, and farmers have high distress levels across the state. Would we expect their organizations to react the same way? The Twin Cities have people living in the streets in the vicinity of the St. Paul Convention Center and areas just off of Hennepin Avenue. What has been their response? Perhaps what is needed is more middle level theory about the role of economic conditions and interorganizational activity.

Economic disadvantage alone does not explain organizational behavior. Reliance on a single variable oversimplifies and may mask the underlying reason for certain behavior. I am not faulting the research because of this, but rather to point out that there is a need to place the research in a more general economic and public policy decision-making model. The vague assumptions need to be replaced with a broader array of variables and possible explanations.

Second, I want to raise a more general question by asking if we do not have the possibility of observing different interorganizational activity and behavior if we observe the same organization in other settings. It would make sense that a crisis situation would bring about different behavior which could be atypical of what usually happens.

Thus the question is whether the contextual setting influences organizational behavior? If so, then one may be able to develop a typology of expected organizational behavior under differing conditions. If this is the case, then one must be careful about drawing general conclusions about an organization's behavior unless all of the various contextual settings have been studied or the conclusions are noted as being relevant to the particular contextual setting that has been studied. Rather than limiting interorganizational analysis this provides a depth and complexity often missing.

Third, I would agree with the need to do comparative studies, but we need to be more specific in what the common characteristics between those studies are and are likely to be. Comparative studies often are difficult because the setting and specific events and organization are likely to differ in some meaningful way. This is not overstating the obvious, but rather pointing out that interorganizational behavior is best understood when the varying conditions under which it takes place are understood. This is an essential step not only in framing comparative studies, but in understanding the limitations of a set of case studies no matter how carefully they have been done.

Longitudinal study may be a more important and useful approach than the comparative one. Here, concerted in-depth analysis permits a thorough understanding of the organization's behavior and change and also provides a useful analytical framework for understanding how organizations vary over time. The major disadvantage is that the observer is limited to one organization that may or may not be unique or that has experienced a unique set of conditions or events that influenced behavior.

The major point is that drawing general conclusions from interorganizational analysis, just as with any social analysis, is usually very difficult and often misleading. Thus, the researcher must choose the design carefully as well as cautiously interpret the conclusions and generalizations set forth when the research is completed.

Turning to J. Allen Whitt's chapter on Louisville and the role of financial interests in urban growth (Chapter 5), let's assume for a moment that Molotch's assumptions about growth and urban centers are correct and that this analytical framework is a useful way to understand interorganizational behavior. Several points need to be made. First, it strikes one most dramatically when one is in downtown Louisville that there is an absence of housing of any type. This is largely a commercial redevelopment. Another striking observation is that the development is haphazard and uneven. Even the successful commercial enterprises appear to be seasonal, and many are not busy on most weekends. If the corporate elite that invested in these developments is attempting to make money, they are not doing a very good job. One wonders if profit was the *sole* motivation in these decisions? Or is it possible that the redevelopment was seen as community investment and not just part of the profit orientation?

Second, it is not clear why Humana as an organization would invest in the Kentucky Center for the Performing Arts as a way to make money. Clearly, the investment was made not just for the economic gains that would acrue. I think the chapter overstates its position and at times offers an overly simplistic view of organizational motivation. This tendency undercuts the argument that organizational behavior is linked to organizational goals. In this case, Humana had more diverse goals than maximizing its economic return.

This is one of the most serious problems in interorganizational analysis. Who determines what an organization's goals are: Does the observer or does the organization through its stated goals? Or does the observer throughout studying what goals the organization actually pursues? What happens when these change? How does one account for it: Is it due to changes in the organization, to leaders' perceptions, or due to the process itself? Certainly the answers to these questions provide a different perspective for all involved.

Three, people who give to the arts are those who also are interested in downtown development. This is one of Whitt's major points. Again, it is not clear why that is so surprising. If one has vested interests in the community to protect, this may be one way to do it. In fact, in prior years community investment of this type would have been seen as a positive act by those with corporate money instead of simply another way to plunder the community for all it is worth. There is the example of Gary, Indiana, and the failure of the steel industry to invest in that community.

The point here is not whether Whitt is right or wrong, but that interorganizational network analysis can be faulty if there are too limiting a set of perceptions as to why organizations behave as they do. Is it not possible that organizations can be as unpredictable and irrational as individual human beings under certain conditions? By stressing only the unidimensional aspects of organizational behavior, this variation in behavior is often overlooked. The result could be a serious oversimplification of the decision-making process.

Turning to Edward Laumann and David Knoke's chapter which is based on their idea of the organizational state (Chapter 2). Their approach provides a conceptually rich basis for this type of research, and they are to be commended for providing such a framework as it helps clarify their major points and, what is more important, helps to provide a conceptual framework to understand the results. Several comments are applicable.

First, the concept of interest seems to be a bit oversimplified. Take the example of a person opposed to filing flight plans because it tells others where they are exploring. If one is a low-budget oil company one might welcome such filings since one could determine where other companies are exploring, or one might welcome such filings if one is a company not exploring in the United States. Clearly, motives and interests are hard to attribute. They can be complex, and they can change as policy developments take place. Thus one may oppose a policy at one point in time and favor it at another. In addition, organizations with similar interests and membership may have very different agendas.

A good example of this changing nature of policy preference was exhibited in the recent tax reform. Large financial institutions who originally opposed tax reform in 1983 and 1984 changed their tune as legislation had special exemptions in it for them. Thus, any general theory has to be able to account for this type of change in policy preferences. How do these changes come about? Present theories fail to account for them.

Second, I have theoretical difficulty with assuming governmental decision-making bodies are the same as private organizations. For example, clearly the White House and Congress are major participants in many of these decision-making events described in the chapter. I am not sure they can be modeled as they are in the chapter.

Take energy, for example. Clearly, there were different points of view within the White House Staff and within various participants in the federal agencies. How do these differences influence policy? The model at times oversimplifies a very complex process and seems to assume that a particular organizational unit has only one set of values and preferences. Empirical evidence would not support this.

Finally, the most interesting question raised by Laumann and Knoke is their closing contention that more normative political theory is needed. It seems that they have supplied that. Their research, while it may be empirically based, has a variety of normative assumptions including an assumption that individual actions do not matter, and that corporate and organizational decisions at all levels are the fodder for the policy process. If one accepts this, then the way one views the world and, even more important, the way one views decision making in the policy arena changes drastically. This is a powerful analytical scheme, but its foundation, at least at this time, rests more on normative assumptions than empirical evidence.

Turning to Eugene Johnsen and Beth Mintz's chapter on organizational versus class components (Chapter 3), it is not really clear why the row and columns of the matrix are manipulated rather than the matrix or a combination of matrixes. This needs better justification or at least explanation.

How do these interacting points move beyond the private sector and intersect with the public? What is the relationship between public and private decision making? These questions need to be considered if the analysis is to have general applicability.

It is not clear what the significance of this analysis is for an increased understanding of the policy process. There is a need to show that these interlocking directorates make a difference in terms of policy decisions both for the organizations and for when they interact in the larger societal setting. In essence, it is necessary to show that it makes a difference and how it makes a difference. It is not sufficient to assume that it does make a difference without sufficient empirical evidence.

In closing, let me add several additional points about the general approach that I think is important. First, all the chapters, to one degree or another, need to be more concerned with linking their assertions to specific policy decisions. Most emphasize the theoretical but lack supporting empirical data. If the goal is an increased understanding of society's policymaking as it is, then more detailed analyses and evidence of the interorganizational impacts are needed. This seems to be a necessary requisite if interorganizational analysis is to become an important analytical approach to understanding policy decisions.

Second, each chapter has some theoretical assumptions. Clearly Laumann and Knoke's chapter is the most developed along these lines, but each could use additional conceptual and epistemological thought. Greater clarity on exactly what power is and is not would be helpful in these considerations. All would be enhanced by a clearly stated definition of power. In addition, the authors tend to view the policy process in very narrow terms. This view excludes other relevant actors and at times assumes that a specific decision solely determines outcomes. There is not enough discussion of policy implementation as an aspect of policymaking which the organization might choose to concentrate on if it felt it would be or actually was unsuccessful at an earlier stage in the policy process. Including the implementation process as part of the policymaking process would strengthen the conceptual and empirical basis for those undertaking interorganizational analysis.

In conclusion, while I agree that interorganizational analysis is useful in some situations and can be a powerful tool for the policy analyst interested in understanding the policy process, I do not think it is the only tool that can be useful or that its use excludes other analytical approaches. Thus the implicit argument that interorganizational analysis alone will tell us what we need to know about the policy process is rejected. Interorganizational analysis, in conjunction with other approaches to the study of the policymaking process, will increase our knowledge, but by itself, it does not have the explanatory power needed to clearly detail the intricacies of the policymaking process. It does hold considerable promise, as these chapters indicate, for an increased understanding of and a different perspective toward the policymaking process. These are considerable accomplishments.

References

Hawley, Willis D., and Wirt, Frederick M. (1974). *The Search for Community Power* Englewood Cliffs, N.J.: Prentice-Hall.

Ingraham, Patricia W. (1987). "Toward more systematic consideration of policy design." *Policy Studies Journal* 15(4):611–628.

Spitzer, Robert J. (1987). "Promoting policy theory: Revising the arenas of power." *Policy Studies Journal* 15(4):675–689.

7 An Outsider's View of Network Analyses of Power

Arthur L. Stinchcombe

Some Traditions in Network Analysis with Different Virtues

First, I would like to comment briefly on where all the study of social networks is occurring. My impression is that the different fields in which network analysis is applied have been growing apart, so that there is no longer much cross-fertilization, neither in methodology nor in substance.

Formal Organizations

My first publications, 20-odd years ago, were in the area of formal organizational analysis. My first two publications concerned the internal structure of organizations as a network of relations among positions, about how statuses could be defined by the pattern of multiple relations among positions (I used the relations "advises" and "commands"—Stinchcombe, 1958) and the structure of relations among organizations in the construction business created by contracts and subcontracts and how that contrasted with the kind of organization built in bureaucratic organizations with stable relations among statuses (Stinchcombe, 1959). Even more current, for example, is my work on the manner in which hierarchical relations among organizations become established in various industries through contracts (Stinchcombe, 1985).

The general point is that the units of, for example, Laumann and Knoke's network analysis of policy domains, namely formal organizations, are themselves networks of relations among positions, which is why they can act. The organizations are themselves often composed of still other organizations linked together in a complex and detailed system of interorganizational governance [studied in detail by Oliver Williamson (1975, 1985) and his followers], contracts and subcontracts, and similar constitutional agreements. For example, the AMA is a network of relations of the Washington lobbying group to constituent state and county organizations, to the AMA's annual meeting, and so on.

The power in such structures is often explicitly organized internally by contractual or organizational constitutional devices, and information flows according to "information systems" with a specifiable long-term structure explicitly organized to transfer the information. The main contributions of this literature are to specify the complexity of the networks *inside* the nodes of other people's networks and to specify the complexity and formal character of a lot of the relationships among organizations in the business world.

In the extreme, the connections between individuals in the networks, or the connections of individuals to political institutions, can dominate the relation of the groups to politics. This is close to Walder's definition of "communist-neo-traditionalism": The independent existence of groups with political interests is illegitimate in communist societies, but of course individuals in those groups have political interests that they pursue through individual links with the party and the state (Walder, 1986:esp. 5–8).

Similarly, academic disciplines constitute dense networks of individuals within universities, and if one meets a highly paid member of, for example, a major university, it makes a great difference which one of those networks inside the university he is in. This means that universities do not speak with one voice on science policy, but with many separate disciplinary voices, which may conflict within NSF; that departments and schools within universities are competitors for power and resources (e.g., laboratory space); and that a department chair embedded in a given network cannot be depended on by the university to minimize the labor cost of producing a given number of semester hours' credit in sociology. The internal network structure of a university means that the university as a unit will not be a powerful actor, as would a corporation or a union of a similar size. This also affects organizations such as the AMA; they cannot speak effectively for the physicians on medical school faculties.

Sociology of Science

Another area in which network analysis had an early start is in the sociology of science. Networks of citations have been shown to have features indicating the collegial interdependence of a group of researchers who continuously exchange information on a given piece of a research frontier, and a larger structure of prestige and disciplinary flow of respect and ideas (e.g., Cole, 1970; Mullins, 1973; Cole and Cole, 1973; Mulkay, 1976; Garfield, Malin, and Small, 1978). One of the most interesting aspects of the research in the sociology of science is that the people who engage in ethnomethodology, anthropological, or historical analysis of concrete interactions also read the formal quantitative network literature, and even sometimes calculate this themselves. Therefore, the formal network analysis has been subject to an anthropological and historical critique of a depth and range unusual in the network literature (e.g., Mulkay, Gilbert, and Woolgar, 1975; Gilbert, 1977; Edge and Mulkay, 1976; Edge, 1979; Cronin, 1981).

Thus, while it is true as Laumann and Knoke (this volume) specify that people in politics are influential primarily because they act on behalf of organized institutional interests, the anthropological data brought to bear in the sociology of science shows that such institutional spokesmanship is an exceedingly complex and nuanced exchange of messages by individual people working in the structure. The outcome of "being a representative of a group" is not indifferent to exactly who says what to whom in what linguistic form.

Human Geography

One of the features of network analysis in human geography, for instance, as represented in the classical work by Otis D. Duncan and his coauthors in *Metropolis and Region* (1960; see also Duncan and Lieberson, 1970) and in Duncan's work *Statistical Geography* (1961) is that the relationships among cities or other ecological entities are typically clearly quantitative, and the quantities can be and are routinely measured continuously over time. Thus distance between nodes (e.g., cities) is a precise numerical variable that does *not* change over time, whereas travel time between the points *does* vary over time. Flows of deposits among banks, flows of newspapers from central publishing places to readers in surrounding cities, flows of wholesale trade in different lines of goods, quantities of physical flows that "break bulk" or are used in manufacturing processes at a given node in the transportation system, commuting patterns, and so on, give multiple quantitative measures of the relations between geographical points.

The structure of relationships among the flows, and how this determines the structure of the social organization at the nodes in the flows, receives its richest statistical treatment in this urban ecology or human geography literature (see also Stinchcombe, 1968; Chapter 6). "Metropolitan dominance" is, of course, a power concept that is derived from the study of such flows. Such dominance changes over time because of changes in the quantitative structure of the flows along the links. No doubt the same is true of debts and equity positions that flow along the links studied by Johnsen and Mintz (this volume, Chapter 3) and Whitt (this volume, Chapter 5).

Public Opinion

Of course the ancient stuff about the flow of information in a mass public, which gave us the two-step flow of communication a generation ago (Katz and Lazarsfeld, 1964:esp. 31–42; Merton, 1949), has not died out. Granovetter (1973, 1974), Beniger (1983), Zaltman (e.g., Zaltman, Duncan, and Holbek, 1973), Coleman, Katz, and Menzel (1966), and others have been actively studying the flow of innovations of various kinds, the patterns of flow of job information, and the consultation patterns through which information on drug problems enters into professional practice.

The central important point about this literature is that different kinds of communication nodes have different structural roles to play in the system. For instance, cosmopolitan nodes translate information from news magazines (or from experience in teaching hospitals) into information in a local community, while local nodes translate information from one particular local person to another particular local person (Merton, 1949; Coleman *et al.*, 1966). Various attributes of the nodes have a causal impact on the flow of information (or of course anything else) through that node.

Obviously some of the corporations studied by Galaskiewicz believe that different things will happen to their money if it flows through one node rather than another on its way to an unemployed person's stomach. They would rather not be taxed, but instead would rather donate money to a church for a food program. But we have not been prepared to study the transformations of the quantitative features of networks in the study of politics, even such elementary features as how much of the money gets to the ultimate beneficiaries.

Miscellaneous

Let me mention a few other areas in which much network analysis has been going on in the last 20 or more years, in ways that have generally had relatively little influence on each other.

There are kinship analyses and related work on formal semantics in anthropology (e.g., Hammel, 1965) (which in turn have very little contact with the more impressionistic network analysis of the relations among myths in the work of Levi-Strauss (1963) except that the Levi-Strauss' myths often have a lot of kinship structure in them).

There are analyses of "bloodlines" and genetic relations among various kinds of relatives in population genetics, for the analysis of which path analysis was originally invented and, therefore, stems back at least to the 1920s. [See, e.g., Appendix A on the heritability of IQ in Jencks, Smith, Acland, Bane, Cohen, Gintis, Heyns, and Michelson (1972) where many of the abbreviations introduced at the beginning are for types of kinships relations for which one has IQ correlations.]

There are input–output tables specifying quantitative relations between industries in economies, in varying degrees of detail, and a corresponding set of derived numbers printed in the cells and in the column and row totals of the input–output matrixes (Leontieff, 1951); here, the nodes are industries and the relationships are flows of quantities among them.

The literature on "public choice" can be reconceived as being concerned with two different structures of networks along which the flow of benefits flow, with "public goods" flowing from the producing centers directly to all potential users, while private or appropriable goods only flow where there are reciprocal ties, that is, where the individual user has paid for the good. The problem then, is to create a network of contributors for the public good, for example, by creating a private tied good to create a reciprocal network (e.g., crop insurance) or by creating a center that can coerce contributions (taxation).

A List of Virtues as Goals in Network Analyses of Power

In the future network analysis of power should proceed in the direction it has gone in the past, but with the virtues of all the different network traditions combined into one. The virtues that we already know, from past successes in different fields, that a network tradition can have are enumerated in the list below.

1. Distinguishing networks inside organizations from those outside organizations, and consequently relations inside organizations from those outside is important because networks inside organizations have different functions and different capacities. We should combine the tradition of network analysis of organizations with network analysis of between-organization arenas.

2. Allowing for some of the complexities in the structure of particular relations in the networks suggested in the literature on contracting, in the agency literature, the transaction costs literature, and the literature on particular industries where networks are the basic form for organizing production, such as construction or American arms development (e.g., Scherer, 1964).

3. Embedding network analysis in a tradition of detailed ethnographic and historical studies of the same relations, the discourse that ensues in those relations, the information that flows from it, the social interactions that do not get recorded in formal network data, as in the sociology of science, to provide rich empirical bases for critique of the network analyses (for an example, see Kapferer, 1969).

4. Development of multiple quantitative measures of the relations between nodes in the network, as is characteristic of human geography, especially quantities of flows and measures of distance, that are at least partly autonomous from the network data itself. We should keep track of those quantities over time, so that the evolution of network structure can be studied. The history of the numbers of representatives of particular groups who work in Washington would be an example; it would show changes in the structures of influence.

5. Specification of the relationships between attributes of nodes in networks (variables such as "cosmopolitan" and "local" in the flow of information tradition) that have a causal impact on how the information that flows through the network is transformed at that node. I suspect that the formal apparatus for doing this will turn out to be a modification of that in input–output analysis in economics.

And more briefly and problematically:

6. Network structures with causal directionality that is temporally organized, such as those found in kinship studies in anthropology, evolutionary trees in biology, etc.

7. Systematic interdependent transformations of the content of flows along network lines, as analyzed in structuralist analysis of myths as originated by Levi-Strauss.

8. Statistical techniques for studying populations of events (or correlations among attributes of nodes) that flow along a given type of link between nodes, such as path analysis in population genetics.

9. Attempts to specify more complete input–output structures as used in industrial breakdowns of the economy, with the corresponding advantages of manipulating a matrix that has to add up to 100% of the inputs in each column and 100% of the outputs in each row.

10. Incorporation of the special points of view of the public choice literature into network analyses, especially analyses of the making of public policy such as those carried out by Laumann and Knoke (this volume).

The Microstructure of Social Networks

Almost all of the chapters here are concerned with the macroscopic structure of networks. It is important to note that the big effects that have been long established in the literature are microscopic ones; variations in one's social relations on a small scale greatly affect one's life. Some outstanding examples of this are listed:

1. When one becomes old and feeble, if there is either a wife or a daughter in one's kinship network it is likely that one will be cared for; having a husband or a son frequently destines an individual for a nursing home (Wright, 1983:99, Walker, 1983:115).

2. In the network of scientific communication, if one studies with a Nobel prizewinner, one is more likely to receive a Nobel prize oneself (Zuckerman, 1977:96–143).

3. In the kinship network, the more children in a family, the worse an individual performs in school; this effect has almost the same consequence as the effect of social class, but social class receives more public attention (Duncan, Featherman, and Duncan, 1972:263).

4. If a health interest group has many people in Washington who work on lobbying and legislation and make contacts with congressmen, senators, and health bureaucrats, it is more likely to succeed than if it has few people, and whose proximity to Washington is limited. More generally, the more people at one's disposal to accomplish an effect across a given link in a network, the more influence flows over that link.

5. In the market for forming kinship links (the marriage market), the correlation between spouses' educations is about as high as the correlation

between occupational prestige (partly computed from the mean education of the occupation) and education (e.g., Duncan *et al.*, 1972:182,263), that is, the pressures on the pair that forms the marriage link are about as strong as the pressures to recruit the most qualified worker for good jobs in the labor market.

6. People with impoverished networks of friends and kin are much more subject to various kinds of deviant behavior. For instance, those who have recently moved to a community are much more likely to batter their children and spouses (Gil, 1973:113; for related data see pages 112 and 122). Students who have many friends who plan to stay in college or high school are much less likely to drop out (Haller and Butterworth, 1960);

7. In the economic sector, the more a firm sells to or obtains grants from the federal government, the more regulations it will be subjected to. The more parts a manufacturer sells to the auto industry, the more it suffers from Japanese competition, even if it is more efficient than its Japanese counterpart. The more a firm buys from and sells to a large number of firms, the more likely it will be that the firm will locate in an expensive, metropolitan area (Duncan *et al.*, 1960), and so on.

8. If a person is on the board of directors of a major corporation, that person is more likely to acquire considerable personal wealth.

My point is that very little attention is given to these particular causal relations on the nodes due to the microstructure of their immediate network environment in the network literature. My perception is that the effect on one's wealth of being on the board of directors of a major corporation is larger than any effect of the macrostructure relating social clubs to board membership; as studied in Johnsen and Mintz (Chapter 3, this volume); that the effect of having many people making contacts in Washington is larger than *where* those contacts are in the two-dimensional network structure located by Laumann and Knoke (this volume, Chapter 2), and so on through the macrostructural studies.

It is also important to note that the same applies to organizations as nodes in a network. Hirsch's studies (1982) of why boards of directors choose members who are also on other boards of directors shows that they do so in order to improve their own functioning, among other things. People who are on other boards have information that may be valuable for the company on whose board they serve, and it is to their advantage to have their own executives serve on boards of other companies. Thus, companies that have interlocking directorates should function better, become wealthier, avoid more problems, etc.

My recommendation here is not to turn from macroscopic studies, partly because some of the effects that have been found in that area are large enough to be socially important. But I think it would be more productive if we integrated our theories of the macrostructure of networks with the causal processes ensuing in the microstructure of those networks that fuel social relations. People's rationality and sentiments are likely to be mobilized by social relations that are close and intense. If we have a network science that ignores that fact it will be largely a mathematical and statistical exercise, rather than social science.

Conditional Network Effects

I would like to introduce my next comment with an example that is an outgrowth from the sociology of science. If one classifies the sciences from more paradigmatic (e.g., physics) to less paradigmatic (e.g., political science) and then classifies placement of students accordingly, then the more paradigmatic the science the *less* likely placement of graduate students is by (1) hiring them in the department where they studied, or (2) regionally specific, so that graduates from Berkeley attend California schools, graduates from Harvard to the New England schools (Hargens, 1969; Lodahl and Gordon, 1972, 1973; Yoels, 1974; Pfeffer, Salancik, and Leblebici, 1976; Pfeffer, Leong, and Strehl, 1977; Hargens and Hagstrom, 1982; MacRoberts and MacRoberts, 1986; for a summary, see Pfeffer, 1981:75–76). That is, the less paradigmatic the science, the more powerful the particularistic network effects.

This suggests a general strategy that, I believe, has rarely been used in network studies in sociology; I will call this strategy *conditional network effects*. Some network structures have larger effects under some conditions than others such that scholars in a field cannot really determine the worth of the work. At the humanities end it is uncertain how one would tell whether a premise is true or not. On the other hand, at the mathematics end, where everything that is submitted to the journal is true, one has only to decide whether it is sufficiently interesting, difficult, or elegant to be worth publishing (or is it worth promoting the author).

There are other examples of conditional network effects. A father's occupation has a much more important effect on the child's social status if the father stays married to the mother; in societies where extended families are the norm, families with large estates have more active and important kinship links at any given degree of kinship distance; bonds among siblings are more active (e.g., they visit each other more often) if their parents are still alive; soldiers who have fought together (e.g., French in Viet Nam and Algeria or Portuguese in Angola and Mozambique) are more likely to have the strength of political bonds to mount a *coup d'état;* immigrants of a small migration stream are more likley to have intraethnic bonds of sufficient strength to pass commercial credit to new entrepreneurs, and so become a commercial ethnic group. That is, the links that form a network are often activated conditionally, so that the overall causal impact of the network is larger under some conditions than others.

John Kingdon (1984) suggests that lobbyists have their effect when they are "riding a wave" of policy readiness. For example, HMOs were an alternative for medical care long before the government mandated that employers provide HMOs as an alternative benefit package. Until the wave of cost-cutting in hospital care became a political objective, the policy specialists trying to promote the HMO case in Washington were not very effective; there was no good reason to mobilize since HMOs seemed merely a utopian vision.

Many times we see that the links among people that constitute a voluntary organization appear to be latent, only to be mobilized by an issue. There is historical variability in the conditions that make networks politically mobilizable. One of these variables is vague, namely, "the times are ripe." Some organizations (e.g., some branches of the NAACP) have memberships that fluctuate wildly as civil rights issues wax and wane in the media.

What Flows Along Power Networks Is Often Persuasion, Not Resources

If one reads, for example, Tilly (1986) on collective behavior in four centuries of French history, it appears as if most exercises of power by mobilized collectivities does not consist of *actually* changing the rewards and punishments of a public official, but instead of *giving them the notion* that their rewards and punishments might change if they do not behave. Demonstrations, popular organizations, riots, and even revolutionary crowds rarely actually hurt anybody, or collect enough money to run an automobile factory for a day, or deliver a given number of votes on election day, etc. Instead, they give the office holder the notion that perhaps that might happen unless some action is taken. Since this can have the desired effect (either give in or repress the movement), the exercise of popular power turns out to be a matter of "virtual movements," or "potential power."

Even when the outcome of a public controversy is a decision by a relevant governmental body, such as making rape between acquaintances as well as rape by a stranger a crime, that, too, is (as all who have studied the relation between crime statistics and conviction statistics are well aware) a "virtual motion" in favor of the decision taken, but whether it will be implemented and effective is extremely problematic. So in some sense the main thing being discussed here regarding "power" in a democratic society is "potential power." Potential power is, 90% of the time, all that is ever exercised. Power *is* persuasion, to a large degree. And much of what that persuasion consists of is convincing people (especially officials) that they are operating under a reward and punishment system when that system is constructed out of a tissue of statement and symbol, promises and threats, rather than out of the movement of real resources.

One might say "What is the difference?" The difference is that the flows of relatively tiny resources among organizations can have an effect totally out of proportion to their actual sizes. This is because the real resource that has the power effect is not the money or other resources that flow, but instead the impact of those flows on the ideas of power holders of what they are up against. It is also because the exercise of power consists of a more or less mythical story that affects people's ideas of what rewards and punishments they face in a condition of ambiguity. The more or less mythical flows of resources among organizations are very often what power actually consists of. Potential power and actual power are the same thing and *are* the network phenomenon itself, rather than some "outcome" affected by the resources mobilized.

To be more specific, the reason that Galaskiewicz (this volume, Chapter 4) reports that organizations that receive resources are more influential in outcomes (while those that give are more influential in reputational studies) may not be because they *use* the resources they have been given. It may be instead *because they were given resources* and, thereby, have been shown to be representative of powerful interests (those that give), and that they are thought to be able to influence the futures of officials.

As a cautionary note on analyses such as the foregoing, let us consider the studies of motivations of officials of the small suburban governments in the San Francisco Bay area conducted many years ago by Prewitt and Eulau (1969; Prewitt, 1970). They found that most of the people in these unpaid legislatures or other unpaid or low paid community offices were not looking for rewards and punishments—they were not interested in political careers, did not particularly want to be reelected, and were recruited into politics (a burden) by being persuaded by their friends. This is a reverse network influence on power, such that only if a person's network can make one obliged will he or she assume power (and the corresponding responsibility).

The result of this is that the structures for mobilizing people to get rewards and avoid punishments in politics, political parties, etc. were not very important in the political lives of these small communities. The people then conducted their politics not by what Jane Mansbridge later came to call "adversary democracy," but by the sort of politics that Mansbridge finds in small groups that believe that political problems should be solved by unanimity—by "finding the right answer" (Mansbridge, 1980). With political officials like these, we would expect networks to be effective almost entirely by their symbolic impact, namely, by convincing community officials that they have a consensual right answer to offer for community problems.

The Growth Machine as a Power Structure

Finally let us turn to Whitt's chapter (Chapter 5, this volume) on the "growth machine" that tries to predict a continuing outcome from network structure. Thorstein Veblen introduced this concept in his essay, "The Country Town" (1923), which was revived by Molotch and his colleagues more recently.

It is important to note here that it is an analytical advantage to have continuing strong interests that can be pursued, among other ways, by politics, which differentiate the population—what economists call an "exogenous variable." A lot of our problem in network analysis is that a network has multiple directions. Causal analysis works best when we know from our theory which way the independent variable is going. If we can identify the people and organizations that have large real estate interests in a particular place and then can identify the political system in which the questions of interest to real estate values are (mostly) settled, then we have one set of network links about whose causal impact we have some strong reason to make specific predictions—they will be links that favor growth over amenity in urban politics. Whenever we find a real estate person with links with another type of organization that does not have real estate interests, we know what we want to look for in that link.

I suggest that we might want to try to find the exogenous forces that bear on some of the differential locations in, for instance, the Health arena at which Laumann and Knoke (this volume, Chapter 2) have been looking. Of course, a lot of that may be done in the larger study of which we have been given a sample. For example, the measurement of variations over time and the degree to which medical schools' budgets are dependent on federal monies, or of the proportion of Blue Cross's markets in which they face HMO competition, or the number of hospitals with vacancy rates above what we judge to be the "bankruptcy rate," would give us a handle on who is likely to be exerting influence on whom, for what purpose, and in what direction, at various times.

Exogenous causes of what sorts of influence will be expected to flow in a definite direction along links in the network are a lot of what is needed to make causal assessments in network analysis. Network analysis, as usually practiced, is a picture of things going around in circles, an underidentified system in the econometric lingo. And, as the econometricians have shown us, one cannot usually untangle things that go around in circles without sufficient measurement of exogenous forces. Laumann and Knoke quite often informally introduce these into their systems, for example, by identifying a Catholic part of a network (Catholic affiliation is unlikely to have been created in the short run by community processes); similar informal identification strategies appear in much of the work. We need to pay a lot more formal attention to thinking of, and measuring, exogenous forces that flow through networks as a basis for turning our network work into causal analysis.

Conclusion: Networks as Fixed
Structures versus as Systems of Flows

The overall import of most of these comments is that, just as road systems have their causal impact through the flow of traffic, so systems of links among people or organizations have their causal impact through what flows through them. This flow is determined, in turn, by what the people or organizations who constitute the nodes of the network do to the flow to transform it as it impinges on them, what their interpretation is of that flow for their personal situation, what conditions there are in the environment of the link (or the people in it), and what changes are going on under those conditions. Other determinates of the flow include the size of the resources at the points of origins of the flow, the tenacity and the structure of the links which constitute organizations that occupy some of the nodes, and their internal structure, that either enables them to work in a coordinated way or prevents it, and the like.

The formal analysis of the structure of flows is much more primitive than that of the structure of graphs because it is an odd mixture of finite and continuous mathematics. This has tended to mean that the substance that people study when they are concentrating on particular links (e.g., whether men or women give care to an old person linked to both) is different from the very abstract substance they can study when they are viewing the whole structure of the graph. There is no convenient mathematics and, consequently, no usable quantitative methodology to grasp the fact that the gender of a node transforms the amount of the flow of care along a link that it begins, when one is dealing with a large network structure. So what we know about the Crow kinship nomenclature is something different, something much more airy and abstract, than what we know about care giving for old people. Similarly, the anthropology of astronomy will show that the citation to the work of the director of one's observatory has quite a different symbolic content, and quite a different amount of flow along the link, than citations to workers in other observatories. But this will not necessarily manifest clearly in the clustering of the graph of citations.

I believe that the comments and suggestions here can be reformulated as calling for the development of systematic and transferable methods for analyzing the structure of the qualities and quantities of flows along links in networks. In the meantime, it is a signal to not to be blinded by the poverty of our mathematical competence and to be alert to what is the substantive nature of the causal influences that flow along our networks, even if we cannot calculate what that means structurally. And, as always, such advice leads immediately to the recommendation to seek out the big causes, in this case the influential things that flow along network links toward and away from centers of power.

References

Beniger, James (1983). *Trafficking in Drug Users: Professional Exchange Networks in the Control of Deviance*. Cambridge: Cambridge University Press.

Cole, Jonathan R. (1970). "Patterns of intellectual influence in scientific research." *Sociology of Education* 43:377–403.

Cole, Jonathan R., and Cole, Stephen (1973). *Social Stratification in Science*. Chicago: University of Chicago Press.

Coleman, James S., Katz, Elihu, and Menzel, Herbert (1966). *Medical Innovation: A Diffusion Study*. New York: Bobbs-Merrill.

Cronin, Blaise (1981). "The need for a theory of citing." *Journal of Documentation* 37(1):16–24.

Duncan, Otis D. (1961). *Statistical Geography: Problems in Analyzing Areal Data*. New York: Free Press.

Duncan, Beverly, and Lieberson, Stanley (1970). *Metropolis and Region in Transition*. Beverley Hills, Calif.: Sage.

Duncan, Otis D., Featherman, David L., and Duncan, Beverly (1972). *Socioeconomic Background and Achievement*. New York: Seminar Press.

Duncan, Otis D., Scott, W. Richard, Lieberson, Stanley, Duncan, Beverly, and Winsborough, Halliman H. (1960). *Metropolis and Region*. Baltimore: Johns Hopkins Press.

Edge, David (1979). "Quantitative measures of communication in science: A critical review." *History of Science* 17:102–34.

Edge, David, and Mulkay, Michael J. (1976). *Astronomy Transformed: The Emergence of Radio Astronomy in Britain*. New York: John Wiley and Sons.

Elakana, Yehuda, Lederberg, Joshua, Merton, Robert K., Thackray, Arnold, and Zuckerman, Harriet, eds. (1978). *Toward a Metric of Science: The Advent of Science Indicators*. New York: John Wiley.

Etzioni, Amitai (1961). *Complex Organizations: A Sociological Reader*. New York: Holt Rinehart & Winston.

Finch, Janet, and Groves, Dulcie, eds. (1983). *A Labor of Love: Women, Work, and Caring*. London: Routledge and Kegan Paul.

Garfield, Eugene, Malin, Morton V., and Small, Henry (1978). "Citation data as science indicators." In Yehuda Elakana et al. (eds.), *Toward a Metric of Science: The Advent of Science Indicators* New York: John Wiley.

Gil, David G. (1973). *Violence against Children*. Cambridge, Mass.: Harvard University Press.

Gilbert, G. Nigel (1977). "Referencing as persuasion. *Social Studies of Science:* 7:113–122.

Granovetter, Mark (1973). "The strength of weak ties." *American Journal of Sociology* 78(6):1360–1380.

Granovetter, Mark (1974). *Getting a Job: A Study of Contacts and Careers*. Cambridge, Mass.: Harvard University Press.

Haller, Archie O., and Butterworth, C. E. (1960). "Peer influences on levels of occupational and educational aspiration." *Social Forces* 38:289–295.

Hammel, Eugene A., ed. (1965). *Formal Semantic Analysis, American Anthropologist* 67(5):Part 2.

Hargens, Lowell L. (1969). "Patterns of mobility of new Ph.D.'s among American academic institutions." *Sociology of Education* 42:18–37.

Hargens, Lowell L., and Hagstrom, Warren O. (1982). "Scientific consensus and academic status attainment patterns." *Sociology of Education* 55:183–196.

Hirsch, Paul (1982). "Network data versus personal accounts: The normative culture of interlocking directors." Graduate School of Business, University of Chicago. Presented to the annual meeting of the American Sociological Association, San Francisco.

Jencks, Christopher, Smith, Marshall, Acland, Henry, Bane, Mary Jo, Cohen, David,

Gintis, Herbert, Heyns, Barbara, and Michelson, Stephan (1972). *Inequality: A Reassessment of the Effect of Family and Schooling in America.* New York: Basic Books.

Kapferer, Bruce (1969). "Norms and the manipulation of relationships in a work context." In J. Clyde Mitchell (ed.), *Social Networks in Urban Situations.* Manchester: Manchester University Press, pp. 181–244.

Katz, Elihu, and Lazarsfeld, Paul F. (1964). *Personal Influence: The Part Played by People in the Flow of Mass Communications.* New York: Free Press.

Kingdon, John W. (1984). *Agendas, Alternatives, and Public Policies.* Boston: Little Brown.

Lazarsfeld, Paul F., and Stanton, Frank, eds. (1949). *Communications Research 1948–49.* New York: Harper and Brothers.

Leontieff, Wassily W. (1951). *The Structure of American Economy 1919–1939: An Empirical Application of Equilibrium Analysis.* New York: Oxford University Press.

Levi-Strauss, Claude (1963). *Structural Anthropology.* New York: Basic Books.

Lodahl, Janice, and Gordon, Gerald (1972). "The structure of scientific fields and the functioning of university graduate departments." *American Sociological Review* 37:57–73.

Lodahl, Janice, and Gordon, Gerald (1973). "Funding the sciences in university departments." *Educational Record* 54:74–82.

MacRoberts, Michael H., and MacRoberts, Barbara R. (1986). "Quantitative measures of communication in science: A study of the formal level." *Social Studies of Science* 16:151–172.

Mansbridge, Jane (1980). *Beyond Adversary Democracy.* Chicago: University of Chicago Press.

Merton, Robert K. (1949). "Patterns of influence: Cosmpolitans and locals." In P.F. Lazarsfeld and F. Stanton (ed.), *Communications Research 1948–49.* New York: Harper and Brothers.

Merton, Robert K. (1968). *Social Theory and Social Structure: 1968 Enlarged Edition.* New York: Free Press; London: Collier Macmillan.

Mulkay, Michael (1976). "The mediating role of scientific elites." *Social Studies of Science* 6:445–470.

Mulkay, Michael, Gilbert, G. Nigel, and Woolgar, S. (1975). "Problem areas and research networks in science." *Sociology* 9:187–203.

Mullins, Nicholas (1973). *Theories and Theory Groups in Contemporary American Sociology.* New York: Harper and Row.

Pfeffer, Jeffrey (1981). *Power in Organizations.* Boston: Pitman.

Pfeffer, Jeffrey, Leong, Anthony, and Strehl, Katherine (1977). "Paradigm development and particularism: Journal publication in three scientific disciplines. *Social Forces* 55:938–951.

Pfeffer, Jeffrey, Salancik, Gerald R., and Leblebici, Huseyin (1976). "The effect of uncertainty on the use of social influence in organizational decision making." *Administrative Science Quarterly* 21:227–245.

Prewitt, Kenneth (1970). "Political ambitions, volunteerism, and electoral accountability." *American Political Science Review* 65(1):5–17.

Prewitt, Kenneth, and Eulau, Heinz (1969). "Political matrix and political representation.

Prolegomenon to a new departure from an old problem." *American Political Science Review* 63(2):427–441.

Scherer, Frederic M. (1964). *The Weapons Acquisition Process: Economic Incentives*. Boston: Division of Research, Graduate School of Business Administration, Harvard University.

Stinchcombe, Arthur L. (1958). "On the use of matrix algebra in the analysis of formal organizations." *Berkeley Journal of Sociology and Social Institutions*, 4:56–65.

Stinchcombe, Arthur L. (1959). "Bureaucratic and craft administration of production." *Administrative Science Quarterly*, 4:168–187.

Stinchcombe, Arthur L. (1968). *Constructing Social Theories*. N.Y.: Harcourt-Brace-Jovanovich.

Stinchcombe, Arthur L. (1985). "Contracts as hierarchical documents." In A. Stinchcombe and C. Heimer (eds.), *Organization Theory and Project Management: Administering Uncertainty in Norwegian Offshore Oil*. Bergen: Norwegian University Press, pp. 121–171.

Stinchcombe, Arthur L. (1986). *Stratification and Organization: Selected Papers*. Cambridge: Cambridge University Press.

Stinchcombe, Arthur L., and Heimer, Carol A. (1985). *Organization Theory and Project Management: Administering Uncertainty in Norwegian Offshore Oil*. Bergen: Norwegian University Press.

Tilly, Charles (1986). *The Contentious French*. Cambridge, Mass.: Harvard.

Veblen, Thorstein (1923). "The country town." *Absentee Ownership and Business Enterprise in Recent Times,* Chapter 7.

Walder, Andrew G. (1986). *Communist Neo-Traditionalism: Work and Authority in Chinese Industry*. Berkeley, Ca.: University of California Press.

Walker, Alan (1983). "Care for elderly people: A conflict between women and the state." In J. Finch and D. Groves (eds.), *A Labor of Love: Women, Work, and Caring*. London: Routledge and Kegan Paul, pp. 106–128.

Williamson, Oliver (1975). *Markets and Hierarchies*. New York: Free Press and London: Collier MacMillan.

Williamson, Oliver (1985). *The Economic Institutions of Capitalism*. New York: Free Press; London: Collier MacMillan.

Wright, Fay (1983). "Single careers: Employment, housework, and caring." In J. Finch and D. Groves (eds.), *A Labor of Love: Women, Work, and Caring*. London: Routledge and Kegan Paul, pp. 89–105.

Yoels, William C., and Yoels, Brenda G. (1974). "The structure of scientific fields and the allocation of editorships in scientific journals: Some observations on the politics of knowledge. *Sociological Quarterly* 15:264–276.

Zaltman, Gerald, Duncan, Robert, and Holbek, Jonny (1973). *Innovations and Organizations*. New York: John Wiley and Sons.

Zuckerman, Harriet (1977). *Scientific Elite: Nobel Laureates in the United States*. New York: Free Press; London: Collier MacMillan.

Subject Index

Actor-event interface, within national policy domains defined, 31
Agenda, 29
American Medical Association, 119
Attentive public, 29
"bit-players," 44
nonmembers, 27
Autonomy, 57, 84
of state, 22

BART (Bay Area Rapid Transit), 100–101

Capitalism, 57
Central Intelligence Agency, 2
Civic boosterism, 99
Coalition cleavage, 42
controversy, 48
Community decision-making, 83, 85
nondecision-making, 106
Community influence, 84, 85
and structural autonomy, 84
Corporate director networks, 60–61
national, seminational, and regional, 61–62

Domain. *See* policy domain
Dual of the corporate network, 60

Economic resources, centralization of, 6
Elite (or state) decision making, 58
contrasted with other approaches, 18–22
defined, 18, 21–22
key state policy actors, 23, 24
Elite status, 62

Federal government, involvement in economy and society, 6–7, 22
FLOC (Farm Labor Organization Committee), 8–9
Frame negotiation, 42, 48

Growth machine, 97–99, 128–129
Growth politics, 99, 102–103
and the arts, 103–104
Guatemala
overthrow of government, 2
role of United Fruit Company, 2
role of U.S. State Department, 2

Human geography, 121

Inter-American Development Bank, 3
Interlocking directorates, 20, 87
Interorganization leaders, 84, 86
ranking of core organizations, 45
Interorganizational networks, 7, 92, 99, 100
corporate vs. director networks, 59
social control of, 10–13
Interorganizational relations, 1–3
and managerial elite perspective, 23
and resource dependence theory, 6, 957
and social class theory, 6, 9, 58

Legitimacy, 22, 44, 48

Mobilizing resources, 17, 35, 48, 88–90
through interorganizational ties, 82
through overlapping memberships, 89